More Praise for

There's No Place Like (a Nursing) Home

"…Especially appealing is that Ms. Shoff has gone beyond sharing important information on long-term care insurance, and provided sound, vital advice that will help people ensure that they and their loved ones receive the care they need from caregivers that they can trust."

— **Sandra Pierce-Miller**
State of California Department of Health Services
Director, California Partnership for Long-Term Care

"I wholeheartedly endorse Karen Shoff's empowering and confident approach to long-term care planning. In today's health care environment, it is crucial that individuals plan ahead and take control of their decision making. This book should be read by all internists and family practice physicians caring for patients, who will some day benefit from the excellent ideas presented in this book."

— **Eben Feinstein, M.D.**
Chairman, Department of Medicine
Good Samaritan Hospital, Los Angeles, California

"*There's No Place Like (a Nursing) Home* is the quintessential primer on long-term care — a map with a moral compass on how to navigate the treacherous highways of growing old, ill or infirm, while still staying in the driver's seat for the distance. Karen Shoff's knowledge is matched by her compassion: ingredients that make this book an authoritative and balanced expert presentation. Indeed, the author is an 'inside expert' on a subject that every one of us needs to master. This is not a title that will stay on the shelf: It contains seminal information for consumers and professionals alike.

"This book is a wake-up call — it will make you think seriously about how you want to manage your life after age 55. As so many of our financial assumptions are overturned by changes in the economy, it becomes imperative to take charge of our affairs. *There's No Place Like (a Nursing) Home* walks you through the realities of the average nursing home experience, providing a graphic and chilling factual explanation of why nursing homes represent the most restrictive environment for care (and poor economic value, to boot!).

"In happy contrast, the author offers hope by debunking the myths of home care and long term care insurance, giving you all the information you need to make informed decisions about what is best for *you*. It is very much a book about self-determination and empowerment. Autonomy in your senior years? Now it's possible.

"I salute Karen Shoff's courage in writing a vital book whose time has come, and for her generosity in sharing her encyclopedic fund of knowledge with the public."

— **Hannah M. Nelson, R.N.**
Chief of Staff
Jacobi Medical Center, New York

THERE'S NO PLACE LIKE ~~A NURSING~~ HOME

4 Powerful Steps
That Will Change Your Life

THERE'S NO
PLACE LIKE
~~A NURSING~~
HOME

Karen Shoff
MSW, MSG, LUTCF

InvisibleInk

ISBN 0-9716847-0-7
Library of Congress Control Number: 2002113934

Invisible Ink Publishing
1302 Ozone Ave.
Santa Monica, CA 90405

www.LongTermCareLA.com

To my wonderful parents,

Morris and Freda Sommer

may they rest in peace,

whose loyalty to family was unsurpassed,

and who lived their lives in dignity.

HOW TO USE THIS BOOK

Every effort has been made to make this book as friendly and useful as possible, with the inclusion of forms, sample letters, and answers to many commonly asked questions. As an added feature, we have left extra width in the margins; in these margins, you can jot down any questions, ideas, or follow-up plans you think of… then just turn down the corner of the page, and keep reading. In this way, you won't lose your train of thought, and you also won't lose your great ideas and important questions! After reading a section, go back and find your notes. Many of your questions will already have been answered; items you still feel require clarification or action can be managed easily.

I strongly urge that you schedule meetings with qualified professionals as soon as you read the relevant sections. For example, call to make an appointment with a long term care insurance specialist while you read Step One; schedule a meeting with a financial planner or lawyer while reading Step Three, and so on. Even if the appointments do not take place for several weeks, you won't lose momentum in your planning, or neglect to take care of important items.

Better five years too soon than five minutes too late!

∽

Remember that long term care insurance, tax law, and financial planning are complex specialties that are continually evolving. For updates to the information in this book, and for help in finding professional geriatric care managers, elder care lawyers, and other experts in your area, please visit our site at /www.LongTermCareLA.com/. You are also welcome to contact me directly at Karen@LongTermCareLA.com or by calling (310) 581-8080.

∽

To protect their privacy, I have substantially changed the names
and other identifying details of people whose stories are shared in this book.

Acknowledgments

Thank you, Michael Levin, for encouraging me to write this book after my father passed away. Your hard work and good cheer helped make this book a reality, and kept me going. Ben Gasner understood my message and distilled it far better than I could, myself. His professional focus has made the cover of this book an expressive reflection of its contents.

I am particularly grateful to Judy Gruen for her ongoing writing and publishing advice, and to Roger Woodson (Lone Wolf Publishing) for graciously sharing his professional experience and expertise with me. Gaby Wenig's insights and assistance have been of enormous value. I thankfully acknowledge the assistance of: Martin Abram; Robert Adamich; Sharon Bluestein; Elizabeth Danziger; Martin Kane, Esq.; Dr. Ellen Langer; Ruth Levine; Ira Mehlman; Harry and Michelle Medved; Sarah Shapiro; Nadine Staffenberg; Claude Thau; and Brenda Koplin.

Additionally, my thanks go to the many professional colleagues who offered their expertise, and/or reviewed portions of the manuscript: Steven Barlam, MSW, LCSW, CMC; David Donchey, CLU; Anne Hanssen, MSG; Rabbi David Lapin; Michael Medved; Cheryl and Ferd Mitchell, attorneys-at-law; Steven Moses; Caren R. Nielsen, attorney-at-law; David Rosenfeld, JD, MSW; Wanda Schenk, CPA; Jesse Slome; Judy Tobenkin, MS, MSG; Dr. Lenore J. Weitzman, Ph.D.; and Steven Zarit, Ph.D. Thank you, Sarah Weber, for your insights.

On a more personal note, my family has contributed tireless support, encouragement, and fabulous team spirit: Dr. Allan Shoff, my husband and business partner, did much of the work needed to bring this book to publication; Sarah Lipman, my daughter, provided editing, layout design and advice; Elchanan Shoff, my son, shared his many fine ideas and belief in my work; Robert Lipman, my son-in-law, brought the good sense and good humor to make every task more manageable; and my grandchildren, Basya, Baruch, Shalva, Nosson, and Rina… God-given blessings who bring me happiness.

TABLE OF CONTENTS

HOW TO USE THIS BOOK 8

ACKNOWLEDGMENTS 9

Preface:
LIVING LIFE AS YOU CHOOSE 15

Chapter 1:
FOUR KEY CAUSES OF NURSING HOME PLACEMENT 16

> C = Crisis ❖ B = Burnout ❖ S = Savings Depletion ❖ The Unanticipated Risks of Assisted-Living Facilities

Chapter 2:
NURSING-HOME HOSTAGES 22

> Sarah's Story ❖ The Institution ❖ The Aesthetics ❖ The Horror Stories ❖ There's No Place Like Home

Chapter 3:
BRINGING MY FATHER HOME 33

Chapter 4:
THE FOUR-STEP SOLUTION 37

Step One: Long Term Care Insurance

Chapter 5:
A TALE OF TWO FAMILIES 41

> Meet the Wilsons... ❖ The Impact of Fred's Long Term Care Expenses on Fred and Janet Wilson's Retirement Assets ❖ Thinking Responsibly about the Future

Chapter 6:

IS LONG TERM CARE INSURANCE RIGHT FOR ME? **47**

The Twelve Questions My Clients Ask Most ❖ #1 — Isn't Medicare Enough? ❖ #2 — Why Shouldn't I Spend Down My Assets and Go on Medicaid? ❖ You Don't Get Something for Nothing. ❖ #3 — What Are the Odds That I'll Need Care Someday? ❖ #4 — I've Got Money. I'll Self-Insure. ❖ #5 — It's Hard to Spend Money on Something I May Never Need. ❖ #6 — I Don't Want to Pay Premiums for the Rest of My Life! ❖ #7 — When I Get Sick I'll Deal with It. Why Should I Worry about It Now? ❖ #8 — I've Got Great Genes; No Strokes or Dementia in My Family. ❖ #9 — We Have Longevity in Our Family — Why Do I Need LTCI? ❖ #10 — Why Should I Buy Now? ❖ #11 — Why Should I Pay More to Be Insured by a Top-rated Company? ❖ #12 — Why Does Underwriting Take So Long?

Chapter 7:

YOUR COMPLETE GUIDE TO LONG TERM CARE INSURANCE **63**

What is Long Term Care Insurance? ❖ What Benefits Are Covered by LTCI Policies? ❖ LTCI Benefits ❖ The "Elimination Period" — a Vital Aspect of LTCI ❖ LTCI Benefits and Your Taxes ❖ Worldwide Coverage ❖ Premiums — and How to Protect Them ❖ Protecting Your Benefits against Inflation ❖ The "Pool of Money" ❖ Comparing Daily, Weekly, and Monthly Benefits ❖ Certification ❖ A Brief Summary ❖ Variables to Consider When You Sit Down to Compare Long Term Care Insurance Policies ❖ Find a Broker You Can Trust to Keep Your Best Interests at the Forefront

---

Step Two: Geriatric Care Management

Chapter 8:

TAKE GOOD CARE OF YOURSELF **77**

"In Sickness and in Health…" ❖ "My Kids Will Take Care of Me"

Chapter 9:

GERIATRIC CARE MANAGERS — A MOST VALUABLE RESOURCE ...**80**

A Geriatric Care Manager's Success Story

Chapter 10:

HIRING CAREGIVERS 84

Caregiver Interview Sheet ❖ Is Your Home Ready for You?

Chapter 11:

MORE ABOUT GERIATRIC CARE MANAGEMENT.........................92

by Steven Barlam, MSW, LCSW, Geriatric Care Manager

For Out-of-Town Family Members Who Could Benefit from a Local Professional to Provide Supervision, Feedback and Support ❖ For Those Who Want to Do the Right Thing and Are Just Not Sure What That Is ❖ For Families in Which the Siblings and/or the Parent(s) Can't See Eye to Eye on What to Do in Response to the Parent's Needs ❖ For Those Who Feel All Alone in the Process of Caring for an Older Family Member and Want Professional Support and Guidance ❖ What Is Geriatric Care Management? ❖ Who Are the Geriatric Care Managers?

Chapter 12:

THE "DAGWOOD" GENERATION — HELPING PARENTS PLAN 99

Let Your Parents Make Their Own Decisions ❖ She May Look a Lot Worse Than She Feels! ❖ Whose Problem Is It, Anyway? ❖ How You Can Help an Elderly Parent ❖ Facing Reality: Parents Get Older ❖ In Summary…

Step Three: Putting Your Plans in Writing

Chapter 13:

AN ATTORNEY HELPS YOU PLAN 109

by Caren R. Nielsen, Esq.

Advance Health Care Directives ❖ Durable Power of Attorney for Finances ❖ Last Will and Testament ❖ Trusts ❖ Joint Tenancy ❖ Gift Giving ❖ Conservatorships ❖ Get Professional Advice

Chapter 14:

LONG-TERM CARE DUE DILIGENCE FOR PROFESSIONAL FINANCIAL ADVISERS 119

by Stephen A. Moses

A Country in Denial ❖ A System in Crisis ❖ Professional Obligations ❖ Neither Understandable nor Forgivable ❖ What They Don't Tell You…

Step Four: Finding an Ally

Chapter 15:
NO ONE CAN DO IT ALONE 129

Getting Organized

Chapter 16:
REVIEWING THE FOUR-STEP SOLUTION 133

What Do I Do Now? ❖ Getting Organized ❖ Letter Prototype ❖ Better Five Years Too Soon Than Five Minutes Too Late

Chapter 17:
THE GIFT TO YOU, YOUR SPOUSE, AND YOUR FAMILY 138

Everyone Wins

Afterword:
RELIGION AND EUTHANASIA 140

Appendices

Appendix A:
THE HIGH COST OF WAITING 149

The Cost of Waiting ❖ If the Policy Is Purchased at Age Fifty-Five ❖ If the Policy Is Purchased at Age Sixty-Five ❖ If the Policy Is Purchased at Age Seventy-Five

Appendix B:
WHY AN INFLATION RIDER IS A MUST 152

Comparing the Growth of $200 per Day in Benefits Increasing at 5 Percent Compound vs. 5 Percent Simple Inflation

Appendix C:
**WHAT IS A NURSING HOME? WHAT IS AN
ASSISTED LIVING FACILITY?** 154

Appendix D:
**WHY AFFLUENT PEOPLE SHOULD CONSIDER BUYING LONG TERM CARE
INSURANCE**...155
by David Donchey, CLU

Appendix E:
CARE MANAGEMENT TRUSTS 160
by Ferd H. Mitchell and Cheryl C. Mitchell

> Understanding Care Management Trusts ❖ The Personal Care
> Trustee ❖ The Financial Management Trustee ❖ Questions and
> Answers ❖ Issues to Consider Before Setting Up a Care
> Management Trust

Appendix F:
ESSENTIAL PHONE NUMBERS 167

REFERENCES 170

Living Life As You Choose

"I hate it here. I want to come home."

Until last month, John Burns, ninety-three, was a healthy, active man who did all the shopping, errands, and cooking for himself and his wife, Emma. Then he broke his leg.

"John, I can't take care of you at home. You know that. I'm not strong enough to do it myself. Where would we get the money to hire help for you?"

The reality of the situation hits John like a ton of bricks. Emma is right — she can't care for him at home. But two weeks in the rehabilitation ward of the nursing home have made him desperate.

"I feel like I'm in jail! I need to come home!"

Emma visits daily, bringing food, books, and other tastes of home. She watches his feelings of desperation give way to helplessness, and then hopelessness. His vitality, and finally his life, ebb away. Deeply depressed, Emma dies three months after John's passing.

⤳

The strategic thinking in this book will offer you ways to live as you choose, no matter what health problems may arise. You, your spouse, and your children will be free of the overwhelming burden of caregiving, you can stay home, and your assets will be protected. Peace of mind is within reach.

— KAREN SHOFF

CHAPTER 1

Four Key Causes of Nursing-Home Placement

Healthy people don't just check themselves into nursing-home facilities, and with good reason. What goes wrong?

When I speak to clients or groups about long term care issues, I discuss "CBS" (and I don't mean the latest TV shows). CBS is an acronym I use to help people recognize the first three most common situations that overwhelm families, leading to nursing home placement:

C is for CRISIS
B is for BURNOUT
S is for SAVINGS DEPLETION

C = CRISIS

An unexpected medical crisis often triggers a cascade of events that overwhelm an individual and his or her family. Let's take a look at an all-too-typical crisis and its all-too-avoidable result:

> Janine Cook, a widow, lives at home. An independent sort of woman who has many friends, she does the crossword puzzle every morning, watches her diet, and walks three miles a day, rain or shine. She is secretary of her seniors club, makes meals for sick friends, and volunteers in her local church office.

One day, Janine finishes her walk and returns home, feeling somewhat dizzy. She doesn't think too much about the dizziness at first. "If you get to be my age, of course there are going to be a few aches and pains!"

Then she slips on the kitchen floor and can't move. The phone is within reach. She calls her neighbor and explains her predicament. Her neighbor calls an ambulance and Janine is taken to the emergency room.

Doctors discover that she has broken her hip. She comes out of an emergency surgery just fine. Naturally, there's pain, so the doctors prescribe strong pain medication for her. Not only is she unused to pain medication, the resident doctor does not realize that the drug prescribed is too strong for a person her age, and Janine becomes very confused.

The combination of the broken hip and the overmedication makes her appear demented. She's not — she's recovering from a painful operation and has too much painkiller coursing through her veins. But who will tell that to the hospital staff? Alas, no one.

The hospital staff isn't evil; they see a very old, incapacitated person who's not "all there." They just have no way of knowing what a strong individual this is — her superlative general health, her daily walking regimen, and her powerful personal attitude.

At her time of discharge, the staff recommends to the family a nursing home with some physical therapy. They do not feel she is a candidate for a good rehabilitation facility.

Mrs. Cook's children and grandchildren fly in from five different states and are overwhelmed by the sudden change in her appearance. Concerned about the idea of their mother continuing to live at home alone, they decide that the doctors know best: It's a nursing home for Mom.

Janine, still affected by the pain medication, is very discouraged about her broken hip. She doesn't have the energy to fight her entire family and the medical staff.

In the nursing home, little therapy is given to her and the hip does not heal well. Her family is afraid to bring her home. They are unaware of the options available for home care and have no idea whom to call for help, what the costs would be, or how home care could be paid for. Mrs. Cook remains in the nursing home for the rest of her life, which is four more years.

Janine Cook's story doesn't end "happily ever after." The saddest part of this story is that it doesn't have to be this way.

B = Burnout

The second major cause of nursing-home admissions is *caregiver burnout*, wherein the spouse as caregiver finds him- or herself ill, exhausted, and emotionally depleted from single-handedly providing round-the-clock care.

The Andersons are driving home from their fiftieth wedding anniversary celebration when Doris realizes that Dave failed to remember the names of three of their grandchildren and two of their closest longtime friends.

It occurs to Doris that Dave, who has just turned seventy-five, has been forgetting a lot of things lately — phone numbers, the names of mutual funds, even, for one embarrassing moment, the name of their neighbor's dog. These were all minor moments but Doris realizes now that they may be part of a pattern.

Doris persuades Dave to visit a neurologist. The news they receive is not good: Dave is in the early stages of Alzheimer's, and he will be increasingly losing his memory. Doris is determined to help him remain at home and continue to live their lives as normally as possible.

Dave's condition worsens rapidly and he starts to require almost constant attention. He leaves the house and gets lost. He begins to awaken frequently at night. Doris is sleep-deprived, and becomes ill from the stress and exhaustion.

Friends urge Doris to consider a nursing home for her husband. She doesn't want to listen to them. After all, Dave always provided well for her. After so many good years together, the idea of living without Dave scares Doris more than she will admit.

Eventually, however, Doris becomes so physically and emotionally drained that she gives in, finding the best possible nursing home for her husband. Now, she sits with him every day, and helps as she can. She feels guilty about her decision and no longer has a real life, but at least she is able to visit him and still get some rest at home.

S = *SAVINGS DEPLETION*

Savings depletion is when the money runs out long before anyone ever dreams it might.

Sam Greenwood married when he was twenty-five. Mary was the girl of his dreams, a cheerleader who had some success being cast in small roles in the movies. Sam worked hard in a small beauty supply business, and was proud to be able to put their three children through college.

The Greenwoods had little savings, but felt that they could manage in their old age if they were thrifty and if their home were paid off. At age sixty, Mary Greenwood began to have unusual neurological symptoms. Extensive testing showed that Mary had Lou Gehrig's disease, and that her condition would progressively worsen. Sam and Mary were devastated.

Sam increasingly gave Mary more and more care. Eventually he hired some minimal help in order to get some rest himself, and occasionally take a walk or visit with friends. As the disease progressed and his wife's needs increased, Sam found himself struggling to find the money to pay for adequate care. He had completely run through their assets.

> The only way to obtain care for Mary was to apply for Medicaid
> — welfare. After a lifetime of self-support, it was a devastating
> emotional blow to Sam to rely on a government handout.

> Mary's needs were so great that Medicaid could only offer her a
> place in a nursing home. Shattered, and with no hope of any
> alternative, Mary Greenwood entered a nursing home to spend
> the last eighteen months of her life.

The Unanticipated Risks of Assisted-Living Facilities

The fourth major source of nursing-home placement is nearly invisible.

Buried deep within the fine print of assisted-living facility contracts are clauses that most people choose to overlook: Most assisted-living facilities are not licensed to house people with significant health problems. Unfortunately, a large percentage of those who enter assisted-living facilities are forced to leave when their health deteriorates. If they have already sold their own home, there is nowhere to turn but a nursing home.

> Howard was happy living in the residential care apartment he
> entered after his wife's passing, three years ago. One morning,
> while preparing a cup of coffee, he felt his leg give way.

> Recovering from surgery and hospital-acquired pneumonia, he
> was stunned when his son told him that the management of the
> facility had phoned to inform them that Howard could not
> return. Their insurance just wouldn't allow for such a "frail"
> man to live in their facility.

> His home sold, Howard had nowhere to go. Betrayed, and not
> wanting to burden his daughter-in-law by moving in, Howard
> allowed himself to be transferred to a local nursing home, leaving
> his son to pack up his worldly goods for storage. He had assumed
> that the assisted-living facility would be his home for life.

If you think these matters are difficult to read about, imagine *knowing* these people personally. Imagine *actually living through this* with a parent or spouse. Imagine *being* these people. *True stories like these take place every single day.*

It could happen to you, too.

CHAPTER 2

Nursing-Home Hostages

The name "nursing home" connotes a hospital of sorts — a place abounding with well-trained individuals who hold nursing degrees and are able to care for those who are ill equipped to care for themselves. The name itself implies a place full of health care professionals who have studied for a number of years in a college and had to pass statewide examinations before they were permitted to work. It is a name that is meant to inspire confidence in the institution, and for many thousands of Americans it actually does.

Yet the reality inside a nursing home is in no way similar to its name.

> The first day that I worked in a nursing home, Betty, a resident, called me to her room and told me she had cried the night before. She was unable to move without assistance, and had needed to use the bathroom. She called out to a nurse to take her there.
>
> No one responded. Betty kept calling and ringing the bell at the side of her bed, and still no one responded. She started to cry, and for six hours she lay there, crying and calling, obviously greatly distressed. The nursing assistant on duty was oblivious to her pleas, or perhaps was just ignoring them. Betty eventually wet her bed, and then she fell asleep in her own urine.
>
> Over thirty years have passed, and Betty's story still haunts me.

According to most state regulations, there is no requirement that a doctor be on-site at a nursing home. The highest level of professional caregiver that has to be present is usually a registered nurse (RN) as a "director of nursing services" — for eight hours a day, five days a week. Although the nurse might be on call when off duty, for two-thirds of a twenty-four hour period there may be only a lower-level health care provider present in the facility to participate in the hour-to-hour care of the residents. In California, facilities licensed for 100 or more beds are required to have only one registered nurse awake and on duty at all times, in addition to the director of nursing services.

So who does care for nursing home residents?

Nursing homes are the McDonalds of the health care world — employing a roster of unskilled individuals for the lowest possible wage.

Some of these people might be CNAs (certified nursing assistants) who have taken an eight-week course on how to attend to geriatric patients. Others have not done even that. Whether they have completed the course (which provides only very basic training) or not is materially irrelevant, because the job they are given is low-paid, heavy, dissatisfying work.

The sad result is that care is often administered haphazardly or not at all. The minimum wage that CNAs receive is simply not enough to ensure patients the level of attention they deserve.

Most nursing homes operate at maximum capacity to have maximum profits, which means that they hire the minimum number of CNAs required. Under California state law (which is better than most), each nursing home patient is entitled to 3.2 hours a day of care. Assuming that the letter of the law is followed, patients may be left unattended for almost twenty-one hours a day.

For patients who are reasonably healthy and mobile, this might not be so terrible because they can walk around, feed and groom themselves, and go to the bathroom.

For other patients who are bedridden, this is simply not enough care. Patients confined to bed need to be turned every once in a while, so they don't get bedsores. They need to be taken to the bathroom regularly, and receive proper oral hygiene (toothbrushing, and the like). They might need assistance feeding themselves, getting dressed, or shaving. They might enjoy someone taking them out in a wheelchair occasionally. There is simply not enough time in the day to do all those things.

The care in nursing homes is determined not by need, but by staff availability. *In other words, if the staff is not available, then one's needs are not met.*

↤

As businesses, profit is the first and foremost goal of a nursing home (and that is not a bad thing). The reality that nursing home administrators struggle with is that nearly half of their patients are on Medicaid (welfare); facilities receive so little payment for their care that they actually *lose* money for every Medicaid patient they admit. It is completely unfeasible to hire more staff at higher wages who would be better suited to give emotional and physical care, because that would further bankrupt the nursing home.

This translates into hardships for the patients. An assistant might turn a bedridden patient who is unable to move herself in bed. The assistant leaves the ward, and after a few minutes the patient discovers that she is extremely uncomfortable in the position she has been left in. This patient has no recourse. She has to suffer in that position until the next time the assistant visits her room, and that might be hours later. A diapered patient might be left for hours with a soiled diaper until the assistant walks past the room again to change it.

In a facility where people do not have much time, caregiving is handled as efficiently as possible; there is no time to slowly guide patients in attempts to care for themselves. This causes what author and expert Robert Kahn calls *excess disabilities*. A person becomes more impaired than is necessary. People who are given rehabilitation and are then sent home are much more apt to improve than those who are sent to nursing homes — where they often end up bedridden.

Nursing home employment is a revolving door. However, unlike fast-food restaurants, where customers do not suffer if a new person serves them french fries, the constant turnover of staff in nursing homes results in severe repercussions for the residents.

Residents are not able to become close to the staff, because the staff is constantly changing. There is no familiarity with the people who will be helping the residents to perform their most intimate bodily functions. Residents lose all sense of self as their needs are processed by an ever-changing bevy of unskilled and semi-skilled workers.

Thus the term "nursing home" is a misnomer in two ways: The care administered is not *nursing* care, and the constant turnover of staff means that it will never have the familiarity of *home*. A better name for a nursing home might be "unskilled workers' institution for old people." It doesn't have quite the same ring to it, but it is a more accurate assessment of what life is like in these institutions.

Sarah's Story

Sarah put her father (a retired doctor) in a nursing home when his care became too difficult and demanding of her mother. They paid $5,000 a month to keep him in one of the best nursing homes in Los Angeles, and this is some of what Sarah had to say about the experience:

> We had a sign over my father's bed in the nursing home that he needed his glasses on at all times, because he could not see without them. This sign was clearly written in three-inch letters, but to no avail, because whenever we arrived at the nursing home to visit him, his glasses were not on. His caregivers were unable to read the sign.
>
> The television in his room would always be set to a Spanish station, despite the fact that my father speaks no Spanish. I would tune the radio to the classical music station that my father liked, but when I would visit him a few days later, the radio would be playing rock and roll.
>
> The staff shaved my father a few times a week. They could not use his electric razor, because he had been told not to bring it as it would likely be stolen, so they shaved him with razor blades instead. Invariably, they cut him and he would bleed. When they dressed him, they put him in clothes that were too tight, and then they would just sit him in a chair and leave him there for hours, completely slumped over with his head on his knees.

Nobody had bothered to tell the staff that this was not how to care for a dignified man.

The neglect was not limited to his time spent in that chair. The staff decided that brushing my father's teeth on a regular basis was too difficult a task, so they just let them rot. Many of his teeth fell out. We ended up paying extra money for a dentist to come and fix his abscesses, which could have been prevented by regular brushing.

My father's dental problems affected his ability to chew and swallow, but instead of feeding him patiently and slowly, the staff would rush him through his dinner, stuffing his face with the food on his plate. My poor father had to figure out how to handle so much food without choking.

When my father became incontinent, he was placed in a diaper that was seldom changed. We would remind the assistants that he needed to be changed, but if we didn't, they would leave him sitting there in his own filth. We often had to wait forty minutes before someone was able to change him.

At times my father got irritable, and they would tie his hands down to the bed or the chair he was sitting in.

When I think of the way my father was treated in the nursing home, my blood boils and I feel ill, because I did not know any better. I know that having my father in that expensive nursing home was not honoring him, and I intend to make better choices for my own life, so that I won't have to suffer the indignities that he suffered.

The Institution

I struggled for years to find out why nursing homes don't work. The results of my research, especially the work of Erving Goffman, shed light on the matter.

In normal society people sleep, play, and work in different places, with different participants, under different authorities.

Nursing homes, on the other hand, fall into the category of "total institutions" as defined by Goffman in his excellent book, *Asylums*. He defines a total institution as a "place of residence and work where a large number of like-situated individuals, cut off from wider society for an appreciable period of time, together lead an enclosed, formally administered round of life."

In an institution everything happens in the same place, under a single authority, and in the company of a large group of other people. There is a tight schedule imposed by the powers that be, and there is a rational plan imposed by the institution. (Other total institutions include prisons and mental hospitals.)

Goffman highlights the vast experiential rift between supervisory staff and patients (or inmates). The staff is integrated with the outside world, unlike the people they serve. Each group sees the other in terms of narrow stereotypes. The staff controls the process by which patients can see a doctor — or even a television program. Patients are often excluded from knowledge of decisions about their fate. *The institution is considered to belong to the staff, even though it is the patient who pays the bills.*

Goffman describes a process of "mortification" that occurs in these settings. Patients give up many of their roles, and many of their rights. They call for help, and often have to beg for a drink or to go to the bathroom.

There is a vulnerable sense of territorial violation. People go in and out of the room at will. Personal information is shared; staff and visitors feel free to talk about patients right in front of them. Visitors see their humiliation. Simple comforts to which one grows accustomed, like a soft bed, are no longer there.

Goffman reports that people adapt in various ways to being in an institution. Some try to get the maximum satisfaction they can out of the institution, or try to act like the perfect patient. Some people withdraw or regress. Some refuse to cooperate. And there are combinations of all these once a person has been in an institution for a period of time.

Why do people change when they are in an institution? They feel frustrated by their inability to act as they normally do. They feel humiliated by having to beg for things. Normal defenses, like anger, are punished by the staff. They may feel that they have to withdraw just to survive.

A nursing home is bureaucratic in other ways. It can take weeks or months to get approval for the simplest things. My father was briefly in a nursing home, and we decided that we wanted to supplement his diet with over-the-counter vitamins. It took the staff *a full week* to rubber-stamp the request for the vitamins.

> My friend's father had dementia, and he was moved to a nursing home where he was in severe pain. He was not given any pain medication until a week later, simply because it took the staff that long to get approval through all the bureaucratic channels. The man was in great pain for a week because the nursing home staff was unable to help him sooner.
>
> Ultimately, death arrived before the pain medicine.

In addition, it can become difficult for patients to leave once they have been there for an extended period. People who live in nursing homes for a long time can find themselves psychologically stuck there. When offered a chance to go somewhere nicer, they may not agree to go.

> I remember one woman, Eva, who lived in a nursing home where I was a social worker many years ago. She had been in the facility for years and had completely recovered. However, she was not willing to move out! In fact, she would not even leave the floor she was on.
>
> I arranged for a young teenage volunteer to visit her regularly. After they became friends, I had the student take her down one floor. It was a very big step for this patient. Subsequently, she was taken just outside the building. Finally they walked a few blocks. It took *months* to accomplish this!

A truly eye-opening portrayal of the nursing home experience can be found in a *Wall Street Journal* article by a reporter whose parents had spent the last years of their lives in a nursing home.[1]

> Lucette Lagnado writes that her father "was condemned to live in his final days in an ignominious, tormented way, a fate that

he didn't deserve." Lagnado recalls her experience that the administrators were "afraid of nothing" and were "especially skilled in handling generations of distraught daughters and sons [by ignoring] complaints and pleas for improvement."

The symbol for this facility was "the magnificent fish tank on the premises," which was very beautiful yet represented "a front for visitors that camouflages the exceedingly harsh, painful reality for those within." Lagnado writes that her mother "was roused out of bed each day at the crack of dawn, washed and bathed, and lined up in a row against the wall with other sleepy residents …. She was sick and frail, and could have used the extra sleep."

The explanation for the "military-like regimen" — to accommodate a shift change for the workers, which meant that "residents had to be awakened at an ungodly time," 5:00 or 5:30 A.M. She writes, "What we did or failed to do as a family still torments me, nearly eight years after my father's death."

The Aesthetics

A patient in a nursing home will typically be paying at least $120 (and up to $500) a day for the privilege of staying in one. This is a lot of money, when you remember that in most major cities in the world you can get a room in a five-star hotel for that sum. What does a resident get for that money?

He gets to share a room with an unfamiliar resident. "Privacy" can be created in the room through the use of a hospital curtain, which starts several feet below the ceiling and ends several feet above the floor. (Imagine suddenly being saddled with a strange roommate that you had to live with for the *rest of your life*. How do you think you would feel about it?)

She gets a small, narrow closet that is large enough to hang about ten items of clothing, and a small chest of three drawers. The floor is generally not carpeted, but covered in hospital linoleum; the bed is a narrow twin bed with metal sides.

He gets to eat uninspired meals (whether he likes them or not) and participate in uninspired activities in the common room with all the other residents (whether he likes them or not). Nursing home food is like all institutional food — assembled from freezers or industrial-size cans. It is made for the cheapest possible price, and the lowest common denominator of taste.

It is a setup that is inherently undignified, because it assumes that patients have nothing — no lives that came before the nursing home, no preferences or tastes, no possessions that they have accumulated over a lifetime, no sense of self that might make them reluctant to share a room with strangers. The atmosphere is what one expects in a mental ward or hospital, but a nursing home is meant to be a home.

I encourage you to visit a nursing home near you and look around.

Ask yourself: Is this the type of place that you would willingly go to if you had the choice? Do you want to spend the last few years of your life in a place that smells like a public toilet, where your glasses will be stolen, where you will have to sleep in a small twin bed and where you will wear a diaper for convenience? It's up to you.

The Horror Stories

Early on in my career, I was forced to shut down a nursing home. Even by nursing home standards, this place was shocking.

> When I started there, I bought some cheery posters to brighten up the dining room. The next day, the walls were stripped bare by the staff. This was the same staff that fed the residents day-old food, and had locked one patient in a closet all night.

If not for my intervention, this place would have stayed open.

How is it possible for serious infractions like these to fall through the cracks? Nursing homes do not have to account to anyone. Government inspections take place every few years (and homes are usually given advance warning of the inspection so they can "clean up their act" for appearances sake). Unless relatives of residents are vigilant about overseeing care, there is nobody who will make sure that the staff is even complying with government regulations. Most nursing homes are not as bad as the one I shut down, but they can be miserable nonetheless.

When I was a social worker at a nursing home in Connecticut, my employers learned that it was about to be inspected. So they brought over a kiln from another facility in the chain, along with some other equipment for making ceramics, to show the investigators that they actually had stimulating activities for the patients.

In fact, the kiln and ceramics equipment traveled from one nursing home in the chain to another, always arriving the day before a given location was to be inspected. The kiln was never actually plugged in.

～

Although families may feel that a nursing home is the *safest* place to send a loved one, the reverse is usually true.

Nursing home residents regularly complain of their goods being stolen. Whether staff or other residents are doing the stealing is irrelevant, because it is the culture of the nursing home that encourages the stealing. As long as there is no privacy and no sense of self granted to residents, it follows that people will not have respect for one another's property.

Many nursing home residents also get very depressed. They do not receive emotional support from the staff, or the kind of attention that is necessary for people to stay vibrant. The institutional setting is discouraging and they are not used to the food. There is little that the nursing home administration does to alleviate this depression.

I want to emphasize that many nursing homes are well intentioned. Some facilities run by religious organizations have a lot of funding and many volunteers. These are often superior to for-profit nursing homes. Better homes mean to treat the patients well, but inherent in total institutionalization are certain characteristics that are inescapable. Nursing homes will never actually be homes.

There's No Place Like Home

Perhaps your parents are in a nursing home now. Maybe you put them there because you did not have a choice, as they did not plan properly for their future.

There is not much you can do about this. But you can make better decisions for yourself.

Most people plan for financial retirement. We put money into 401K plans, because we know that eventually we will no longer be able or willing to work.

Why do we so rarely plan for our physical retirement? Having all the money in the world saved up is of no use if you are stuck in an institution where your life's possessions need to fit into a two-foot closet. We know that we cannot stay healthy forever: Physical retirement requires just as much planning as financial retirement does.

There are ways to plan and insure yourself so that 100 percent of the care you need — including caregivers, therapists, home improvements and equipment purchases — will be paid for.

Take control of your life, take control of your future, and plan ahead so your last days will be those of peace, calm, and dignity in the comfort of your own home.

CHAPTER 3

Bringing My Father Home

They all told me I couldn't do it. Some told me I was crazy even to attempt it. Imagine taking a severely ill 97-year-old man into your home!

My dear father had just suffered a massive stroke at his home in upstate New York. When I arrived at his bedside the internist told me that Dad had suffered irreversible brain damage and would probably die within the week. He refused to even order a neurological exam, and had ordered that he be given only fluids, but no real nutrition.

I wasn't ready to write off my father so quickly. His lifelong spunk and fantastic attitude were factors that I believed could help prolong his life, and perhaps enable him to recover to some extent.

To accomplish this goal, our family sought the advice of rabbis renowned for their extensive knowledge of *halacha* — Jewish law — and medical ethics. They told us that it was forbidden to deprive a patient in my father's condition of nutritional support. We summoned the internist and insisted he provide both nutrition and a full neurological workup. For the moment, we were holding death at bay.

The neurologist came into Dad's room and said, "Sir, if you can hear me, put up one finger."

My father's finger shot up.

I was thrilled. I knew he still had plenty of life left.

Once the doctor's expectation of a speedy demise seemed not quite so certain, I decided to bring my father to my home in Santa Monica, California, and have his care given in my home. "You can't do it," the hospital administrator warned me. (He was the first in a long list of people to warn me thus.) "Do what I did with my mother. Send him to the nearby home for the elderly."

He was convinced, as were the discharge planners and doctors, that the premise was unreasonable. At the very least, I would suffer the burnout so common in these situations.

I was not an innocent in these matters. I had spent years as a social worker working in and consulting to nursing homes. I knew my father would never survive in one. Of course, I knew I could not give him the actual care myself, but that we would hire full-time caregivers around the clock.

After all the love my father had shown me, I had no choice but to go forward and bring him home. My husband, Allan, agreed: "We have to do it at any cost," he reassured me.

We spent an entire month getting ready before bringing him to Santa Monica. We prepared a room, we lined up a Medicare home health agency, and interviewed and hired our own twenty-four-hour caregivers and other therapists. We found doctors in all required specialties. We set up files for prescriptions, legal issues, medical records, insurance cards, phone numbers, and so on.

We made sure that key staff was present to greet him when he arrived. One of the most exciting moments of our lives was the day his hospital jet from New York landed in Santa Monica.

But at the same time I was scared. Would we know what to do?

We moved him in and got him comfortable. By just the second evening after his arrival, I was exhausted! However, within a few days we had a routine going. Allan did all the shopping for the medicines and supplies. We soon took my father in the wheelchair van service to meet his new doctors.

Our biggest hurdle was how to manage if my father's assets ran out. My father was already too old to buy long term care insurance with decent home care benefits when such plans became available during the 1990s. Nevertheless, my father needed the care and services, and we began to spend down his assets — at a monthly clip of $10,000!

We grew up in a modest home and my father supported us with his retail business. When he came to the United States at age twenty-one, he borrowed (and paid back) money to send for other relatives who were stranded in Europe. Much of the money he had earned and saved was spent on home care for our mother during her later years. In addition, for the two years prior to his stroke, after several serious falls, he spent $70,000 a year for his own round-the-clock care. In short, a significant part of his assets had already been depleted.

My brother, sister, and I all agreed that a nursing home was not an option, although the costs were considerably less. We were convinced Dad wouldn't survive long in a nursing facility with direct care for only about three hours a day. At home, a caregiver is standing by at every moment.

I carefully tried to balance how much to spend on his caregivers, on physical and speech therapy, and on supplies and equipment. I never knew if the funds were going to run out, and lived with great apprehension about what would happen should his assets become completely depleted.

During my many years as a gerontological social worker I never advised a family to adopt the route I followed. Bringing an elderly, ill parent into one's own home is a very personal decision. I have discovered, however, that with the proper understanding of how to use caregivers and care managers to our advantage, and with the proper legal and financial planning years ahead of time, most people can live out their lives in the comfort and dignity of home, even after a serious medical setback.

Our family, friends, caregivers, and doctors experienced great satisfaction when my father's condition improved dramatically early last spring. He enjoyed hearing my sister playing the piano, and our singing at the Sabbath table. He was so happy to once again participate in conversations. He spoke clearly and we listened in wonder as he told us the final stories of his life and shared his love and concern for all of us. He was kind and philosophical, and affected us all with the calm way he handled adversity.

I tried to juggle how much to spend on his physical and speech therapy; and yet I would have felt terrible if he were not to get all the help that he needed, and if he were to have passed away with money left over that could have helped him. So we went forward, praying that his savings would hold out and that the few stocks remaining in his retirement portfolio would hold their value!

I know of families who have decided to give their parents lesser care, often in a nursing facility, in order to protect their inheritance, or in the hopes that there will be money for a college education for their children or grandchildren. I personally believe that people are entitled to have their money spent for the best possible care, and that the family should not withhold this care in their own interests, no matter how laudable those intentions might be.

We felt great joy when the doctors told us Dad was getting the best care possible, and were surprised that his blood work, for such an incapacitated man, could show such good results. (We gave him wonderful vitamins in his tube feedings.) Dad was with us for almost a year, and for a long time he showed improvement following the stroke. We were thankful for each good day.

I know it wasn't easy for Dad to be unable to walk and eat normally. He nonetheless remained so kind, so philosophical, and so concerned about others. As always, he gave a great deal of love and attention to the family and to his caregivers.

Late in May of 2000, eleven months after his stroke, my father passed away. On his very last day a doctor expressed amazement at how good he looked, because of the excellent care he had been receiving.

Those months together were precious to our caregivers, doctors, friends, and relatives — precious to us all.

I have gained a quiet but strong peace of mind knowing that my father was as comfortable as possible, as we shared his last year together.

CHAPTER 4

The Four-Step Solution

Recognizing the kinds of overwhelming situations that force people into nursing homes gives you an enormous advantage: You can prepare for them. There are four straightforward steps you can take that can keep you in control even if things take a turn for the worse:

> *The first step is long term care insurance,* which pays for care after a serious physical or mental loss of ability.

> *The second step is finding a geriatric care manager,* an individual trained to supervise your care if you cannot completely take care of yourself.

> *The third step is putting your desires and needs in writing,* so that should there ever be a crisis in which you cannot speak for yourself, others will be *legally bound* to follow your wishes.

> *The fourth step is finding an ally,* usually a doctor, who understands and sympathizes with your wishes for your care. The purpose of the ally is to lend support to you and your family in any potential struggles with other health care professionals about how best to take care of you.

In taking these four steps, you, or perhaps your parents, will have done everything possible to preserve financial assets, protect the health of family caregivers, and live a life of dignity.

STEP ONE:
Long Term Care Insurance

CHAPTER 5

A Tale of Two Families

We are living longer today. Many older Americans live with chronic illnesses or debilitating conditions that might have been quickly fatal not too many years ago, such as diabetes and heart disease. More Americans need more care for more years than ever before. *Who is going to pay for that care?*

⌒

I'd like to tell you more about John and Emma Burns, the couple you met in the preface to this book. I know their story, because I heard it from their good friends, Harry and Donna Acton.

> Although John was already in his nineties, and Emma was only eighty-six, he was the healthier of the two. Emma's arthritis had already made it difficult for her to function for twenty years. When Emma got the call from the emergency room, telling her that John had badly fractured his leg when he slipped in a puddle outside the local market, she didn't know how she would ever manage her own cooking, cleaning, shopping, and laundry. Taking care of a sick husband was simply out of the question. Emma was just too frail.
>
> There was no possibility of hiring help. John and Emma lived frugally — they managed on their Social Security benefits and pensions, but there was certainly no money for extras.

As John's forced immobility in the nursing home weakened his body and spirit, the stressful situation was affecting Emma as well. Not wanting to further burden him, she never told John about the twinges in her chest, or the dizziness she was feeling every morning. She never told him that she was subsisting on packaged foods. She never told him how hard the daily visit had become.

When Harry and Donna Acton heard that John was hospitalized, they assumed that he would recover and be sent home quickly. It was only when Emma tearfully told them about John's desperate phone calls that they became alarmed. Feeling helpless, they did their best by visiting John in the nursing home, bringing dinner once a week to Emma, and phoning daily.

The deaths of John and Emma hit the Actons hard — very hard, indeed. At the same time, the Actons became aware that they, too, were vulnerable. Already in their late sixties, they weren't sure what they could do to protect themselves, or even how to find out what to do.

While in my office discussing a change in their health insurance policy, Harry discovered that my mother was being cared for in her home back east. He told me about John and Emma, and expressed his own concerns to me. I will never forget how amazed and relieved Harry Acton was to discover that there existed a form of insurance that could protect him and his wife from the financial and caregiving ravages of ill-health: long-term care insurance (LTCI).

I found an affordable long term care insurance policy for the Actons.

> "I hadn't realized how scared I was of getting older until the policy arrived," Donna told me. "When I opened that envelope, every muscle in my body relaxed."

> Two years later, Donna suffered a small stroke, which affected her sense of balance, making it difficult — even dangerous — for her to dress herself, bathe herself, or walk unaccompanied. To Harry and Donna's tremendous relief, their long-term care insurance policy covered the cost of a live-in caregiver to help Donna with her daily living.

Four years have passed. Donna and Harry enjoy good care, good
food, a clean house… and living at home with each other.
Harry spends plenty of time with Donna, but can also go out
alone or with friends without compromising Donna's needs.
"It's a life worth living," Donna says.

Meet the Wilsons…

About two miles away from the Actons live Fred and Janet Wilson. They don't
know each other, but I know both couples. What a contrast.

Fred enjoyed a highly successful career as a stockbroker, also
investing wisely for his own account. At the time of his retirement, he was worth approximately $2.4 million, not including
the value of his home. Fred and Janet, in their late fifties, looked
like they had the world on a string.

In a split second, their world changed. Not long after Fred
retired, his car was totaled by a drunk driver. Fred survived the
accident, but it left him paralyzed from the waist down.
Bedridden and unable to walk, Fred needs round-the-clock care,
regular physical therapy, and a wide variety of equipment and
supplies — the bill comes to over $150,000 a year.

It's been five years since Fred's accident. Fred is only sixty-one. Doctors say that
despite the accident, he's got the same life expectancy as any other healthy man his
age. *In another seven years — assuming Janet remains healthy — the Wilsons will
have wiped out all of their assets, excluding the value of their home.*

The Wilsons are well aware that they run a serious likelihood of outliving their
still substantial (if rapidly declining) resources… and the thought terrifies them.

The financial and physical toll is hardly the only consideration in the Wilson
household:

Fred, for his part, resents being dependent on others to help
him. He hates "wasting" all that money on himself. Secretly, he

worries that Janet might physically collapse one day, or throw in the towel and leave him alone.

All of this has strained their relationship with their three children. Two of their three children have been pressuring Janet to put Fred in a nursing home. They tell their mother that it's really in her best interests. "Your life will be so much easier when you have the freedom to take care of yourself without worrying about Dad all the time." Janet suspects that far from being altruistic, the kids really want to keep the family coffers from being drained. She senses that fear of losing their inheritance motivates the children as much as, or more than, their concern for her own well-being.

The emotional toll on Janet is incredibly high; it's very hard for her to see her once-vibrant husband unable to take care of himself. She finds it increasingly difficult to live with caregivers coming and going twenty-four hours a day. Janet feels that she has no privacy — in fact, she *has* no privacy. She also has no social life. Janet knows that many of her friends have ceased to call because she has been unable to make time for them the past few years.

Janet has given serious thought to placing Fred in a nursing home, simply because she's tired of spending money; tired of pressure from the children; tired of the responsibility of hiring, firing, paying taxes, and managing a small health care staff. Janet, at sixty, simply does not have the energy for this never-ending, all-consuming task.

Without telling Fred, Janet actually made a tour of nursing homes in her area. She did not like what she saw. The nursing homes were simply not an option. Janet knew that Fred would not survive six months in such an environment.

Fred had always been "Mr. Wilson, the highly successful stockbroker" in the community. He was well known for his charitable giving, and for his business success; clients and friends looked up to him. In a nursing home, "Mr. Wilson" would suddenly become "Fred," just one more needy old person in a building full of needy old people.

In short, they have very few options, and none of them seem right. Janet has taken no action. She and Fred still live at home, and their money is still walking out the door to the tune of $153,000 a year... with no end in sight.

What went wrong?

Fred and Janet had once seriously considered purchasing long term care insurance. The idea sounded good. Ultimately they decided not to apply for the policy. They figured that with the net worth of $2.4 million, excluding their house, they could handle any sort of long term care needs themselves. There were a lot of other things they wanted to do with that money aside from paying out insurance premiums.

Take a closer look at the Wilsons' financial situation, as illustrated in the following table. Their initial caregiver costs were $120,000; they're now at $153,000. The chart projects a conservative 5 percent increase in the cost of caregiving each year. (If inflation boosts the cost of wages, these figures will be inaccurate; the Wilsons will pay out even more.)

Fred has been averaging 6 percent growth on his assets, which are conservatively invested. Their spending for the upkeep of their home and for household help has been growing at the thrifty rate of 4 percent a year. Prior to Fred's accident, they were spending $150,000 a year on their own expenses, but they no longer take vacations and, much to their regret, no longer feel they can help their children.

The bottom line for the Wilsons: For people who used to be fairly well-to-do, they're running out of money... and fast.

⟳

The Impact of Fred's Long Term Care Expenses
on Fred and Janet Wilson's Retirement Assets

Fred	Janet	Beginning Value	Yield on Investment	Living Expenses	Caregiving Expenses	Ending Value
56	57	$2,400,000	$144,000	$100,000	$120,000	$2,324,000
57	58	2,324,000	139,440	104,000	126,000	2,233,440
58	59	2,233,440	134,006	108,160	132,300	2,126,986
59	60	2,126,986	127,619	112,486	138,915	2,003,204
60	61	2,003,204	120,192	116,986	145,861	1,860,550
61	62	1,860,550	111,633	121,665	153,154	1,697,364
62	63	1,697,364	101,842	126,532	160,811	1,511,862
63	64	1,511,862	90,712	131,593	168,852	1,302,129
64	65	1,302,129	78,128	136,857	177,295	1,066,105
65	66	1,066,105	63,966	142,331	186,159	801,581
66	67	801,581	48,095	148,024	195,467	506,184
67	68	506,184	30,371	153,945	205,241	177,369
68	69	177,369	10,642	160,103	215,503	(187,595)

Thinking Responsibly about the Future

Nobody wants to grow old. Nobody wants to get sick, or have their parents get sick. Yet avoiding an issue won't make it go away. The story of Fred and Janet speaks for itself.

How much would it be worth to you to know that neither you nor anyone else you love and care for will ever have to face the loss of dignity, respect, and freedom that institutionalization entails?

Long term care insurance is actually an investment in your future happiness. It offers the possibility of protecting your health, your family, your financial net worth, and your peace of mind.

CHAPTER 6

Is Long Term Care Insurance Right for Me?

My clients often say, "We'd like to know more about long term care insurance before we decide if a policy is right for us. We think long term care insurance might be a good idea, but we still have some questions about it."

The Twelve Questions My Clients Ask Most

Maybe you have some questions, too. Here are the twelve questions my clients ask most often, along with my answers to them:

#1 — Isn't Medicare Enough?

Medicare is connected with Social Security. When one turns sixty-five it gives medical benefits, and pays doctor and hospital bills.

Medicare is designed to help pay for care that is professional and medically necessary. It pays for a nursing home only following a hospitalization of at least three days, and where skilled care is needed. While it *can* pay for up to 100 days in a Medicare certified facility, it generally pays for less than one month. Medicare also will pay for some skilled home health care services following a hospitalization; for a very limited time (usually one to two months) it can provide a nurse or physical, speech, or occupational therapist. Medicare home health benefits have become more and more restrictive over the last several years.

Medicare Supplement ("Medigap") policies "top off" Medicare benefits. They generally follow the Medicare rules; Medigap policies *do not* pay for anything that Medicare doesn't already cover. Medigap policies *do* help pay your share of Medicare services that are not 100 percent covered.

On average, for long term care required for more than ninety days, Medicare pays only 2 percent. That means the other 98 percent has to come out of your pocket!

#2 — Why Shouldn't I Spend Down My Assets and Go on Medicaid?

There are those who suggest that people divest themselves of all their assets in order to qualify for Medicaid. They say, "Give away your money to your children, and then after several years you can qualify for Medicaid [welfare] without having to spend your own money for care."

This advice is ethically dubious (see the chapter titled "Long Term Care Due Diligence for Professional Financial Advisers" later in this book; better yet, show the chapter to your financial adviser).

Regardless of how people feel about the morality of such a decision, they are likely to discover that *being on Medicaid is not the way to achieve a life of dignity.*

What kind of care will you get on Medicaid? In California, MediCal (California's name for Medicaid) pays very little for home care. You will receive care in a nursing home that agrees to take MediCal payments, but it will not cover the cost of round-the-clock care at home. (Medicaid benefits vary from state to state and even from county to county.)

Also, consider what can happen if you voluntarily give up your assets to others…

> Perhaps your son will go through a divorce. His ex-wife may keep a percentage of the funds you have given them. If your son remarries, his new wife might not be willing to part with such a substantial sum of money just to take care of you.

Or it happens that your daughter has some financial reverses and cannot give you back any of the money, if you decide you want to recuperate at home. Perhaps she is willing to pay for some of your care, but not at the high cost of round-the-clock home care. Her accountant may pressure her to cover only the cost of a nursing home. After all, he doesn't want her to use up all of her funds.

You Don't Get Something for Nothing.

Furthermore, in some states Medicaid does not cover assisted living facilities (as is the case with California's MediCal). *If you desire to be in such a facility in one of those states, you pay for it yourself. Not an easy thing to do if you have impoverished yourself!* If you go on welfare, you may not be able to keep your own doctor, especially if you are in a nursing home.

Medicaid pays very low daily rates to nursing homes. As a result, many nursing home chains are bankrupt. *During the year 2000, 11 percent of the nursing home chains in America declared bankruptcy!* The nursing home of your choice that is conveniently located may not want to accept you, since Medicaid pays them so little. If they can get a private paying patient instead, they would prefer to do so! You will most assuredly have to share your room… and you will have no say about with whom you are to live.

If you are determined to live out your life at home, you need to protect your assets for *your own* possible future use. One never knows how long an illness or disability can last.

Do not divest your assets. Do take the steps necessary to protect yourself.

#3 — What Are the Odds That I'll Need Care Someday?

No one really knows. Does that shock you? The *Wall Street Journal* (October 22, 2001) predicts that more than 50 percent of all Americans will need some form of long term care — either home care, or institutional care — at some point in their lives, based on research by the Health Insurance Association of America.[2] The real figures probably reach as high as 60 or even 70 percent of all Americans, considering the many who receive care at home (from spouses, children, or house-keepers) and are not accounted for by statistics.

Some people decide to buy three years of LTCI benefits, assuming that it is the average length of need. It only represents, however, the average amount of time spent in nursing homes.

The average stay in a nursing home is 2.9 years. But that doesn't mean the average need for care is only 2.9 years — it's probably much longer! Many of those people who went to nursing homes had assistance for a long time at home or in an assisted living facility before they ever reached the nursing home.

Studies show that people who live at home have longer life spans. Their lives at home are not only more dignified, but happier and healthier. One likely reason that the average care need in nursing homes is shorter than the care need at home, is simply that people who stay home live longer. If you receive care at home, you will very likely live much longer than you would in a nursing home, and you need to insure with that in mind.

So what are your odds of needing care? High. Whatever statistics you see tend to be conservative (and they are high enough). If you can afford to pay for lifetime benefits, do so. Otherwise, do your best to get coverage for as long a period as is possible, within your budget.

#4 — I've Got Money. I'll Self-Insure.

Is self-insuring the best option? Not always.

If this is your intention, you should decide how much you need to set aside solely for this purpose in order to meet whatever long term care costs may arise for you and your spouse. This amount will need to sustain you for as many years as either or both of you might require.

If you require round-the-clock care (with a caregiver awake at night), you have to consider $150,000 for *each year* that *each of you* may require care for an undetermined amount of time. This fund should inflate with at least a compound 5 percent inflation per year until the money is needed.

You cannot access this self-insurance money during your healthy lifetime, for you never know when you will need it, or how much care will cost, and you don't want to deplete the fund.

Those who have a realistic option to self-insure are quite wealthy. They are accustomed to living in a nice home, elegant cuisine, and enjoying the finer things in life. They will want good-quality care if they need it. They will also want honest and caring help, as well as plenty of therapy if required, so that they will be able to recover as much function as possible.

Many of my clients have millions of dollars in assets, and could self-insure if they so choose. Why do they buy long term care insurance?

• *They do not want to set vast sums of money aside solely to protect possible future long term care needs.* They want to enjoy their retirement years. Some take big trips with their children and grandchildren, creating lifetime memories for all of them. They want to give gifts to family. They support grandchildren in private schools and colleges. Many give to charities. They are not willing to give up these pleasures simply because they must protect the money for care for some future rainy day. Yet they do want to know that they will be able to get the best care, if needed. So they buy long term care insurance. It is easier for them to pay an annual premium and attain peace of mind knowing that they have protected their assets and care needs, while also still having sufficient money available to enjoy life.

• *It is difficult to spend large sums of money on one's own needs.* Another reason that wealthy people buy LTCI is that they know themselves! Many people become rich by carefully watching their money. They have never spent freely; even though they have plenty, they may not allow themselves the pleasure of using it to obtain the best care for themselves. They might not enjoy as good a state of health as they would if covered by a long term care insurance policy.

> One elegant and wealthy older woman I know hesitates to get
> the best care for herself. Why? Because although she has plenty
> of money, she does not like to spend so much on herself.

• *Insuring avoids family pressure to reduce costs.*

> What if your spouse predeceases you and you become unable to
> handle your own affairs? Your children are now in charge and

want you to have good care, but they never imagined how much it could cost. They had always felt secure that someday they could look forward to a significant inheritance. Now they have a choice: They can spend your own money for good care at home for you… or they may decide that the care at home is an unnecessary luxury, and put you in a nursing home.

Realistic people recognize that this dilemma could be completely avoided with insurance that pays for the cost of the best possible care, protecting the inheritance of their children.

Although your own assets could be used to pay the cost of rebuilding your home in the event of fire, you probably have fire insurance. Your savings could even pay the cost of health care if you found yourself in a car accident, yet you probably also have health insurance. Many people even resent spending money on deductibles and medications.

You are insured for these situations, which is all the more reason to consider insurance for long term care — a situation that can be financially devastating. With this protection in place, you can look forward to enjoying your retirement without fear.

﹏

The cost of care at home depends, of course, on how much help you need. But it's probably a lot more than you would have suspected. Will you sleep all night and let a caregiver sleep too? Will you need help more than once at night? If so, you may well need one day person and one night person.

The following are current rates in my home city of Los Angeles, California. Rates in other regions of the country vary. If you hire directly, anticipate spending at least $100 per day for a live-in or $8 to $12 per hour for an hourly caregiver. Taxes and workers' compensation will be your responsibility.

If you go through an agency that uses its own employees and pays the taxes, estimate $150 to $200 per day for live-in and $15 to $20 per hour for hourly employees.

You also may want a housekeeper to live in who will handle the laundry and cleaning, and also be available as a second set of hands for heavier tasks, such as moving or bathing the patient. Estimate $350 to $400 per week in Southern California for this type of backup.

The following additional costs may need to be taken into account when estimating the costs of long-term home health care:

- Private speech, occupational or physical therapy (Medicare pays only for a very limited period of time).
- Supplies not paid for by Medicare such as incontinence needs, mouth swabs, and related items.
- Equipment not paid for by Medicare such as bathroom equipment, geriatric chairs, and so forth.
- Medications — if you require intravenous medications, this can cost $100 to $200 per day.
- A geriatric care manager, if there is no family member to do the job. This generally costs $100 an hour.

In all, it can cost $300 to $500 a day for round-the-clock care at home (double that amount for care by registered nurses) following a major stroke or other incapacitating medical problem.

For the most part, even affluent individuals should purchase long term care insurance. (For more on this subject, see David Donchey's article later in this book.)

#5 — It's Hard to Spend Money on Something I May Never Need.

True enough. The average age of individuals who purchase long term care insurance is sixty-seven, and is going down. The average age of claimants is getting closer to eighty. This means that most current long term care policyholders can expect to hold their policy for thirteen years or more before they might actually need benefits. It is possible that you may never need the benefits of your long term care insurance (although it is estimated that 70 percent of policyholders will use their benefits someday).

It's worth considering, however, the psychic benefits you will enjoy during the time that you are paying for the premiums on the policy. By "psychic benefits," I mean the peace of mind you gain knowing that were there an unfortunate event or illness, you, your family, and your assets would be protected.

You will sleep soundly knowing that the uncertainty and huge financial risk you face in the absence of a policy have been dealt with responsibly. *There is an enormous amount of comfort derived from the knowledge that you will never become a burden to your family.*

Seventy percent of people with long term care insurance use nonprofessional help, such as home health aides and homemaker services. The ability to get that care through long term care insurance is often the difference between remaining at home versus going to an institution.

It means that you will be able to "just be together" with your spouse and loved ones, enjoying each other's company, instead of relying on them for your cooking, feeding, bathing, dressing, and so on. Caregivers can perform all these tasks, and your long term care insurance can absorb the cost.

#6 — *I Don't Want to Pay Premiums for the Rest of My Life!*

I have good news for you: You don't have to pay premiums for the rest of your life! If you are young enough, you may be able to choose a policy that requires premiums *for just ten years*. Many people who are in their forties or fifties decide to pay out a larger premium for ten years, and be done with it.

This is especially popular among business entities. People who own C-corporations can get an above-the-line tax deduction on tax-qualified long term care insurance premiums (speak with your accountant or financial adviser). This further reduces the cost of the insurance, and makes the concept very appealing. Some people prefer to purchase an annuity that will pay out the amount required to pay their premium each year.

If you buy the usual plan requiring ongoing premium payments and need to file a claim to start receiving benefits, *most good contracts will waive your premium costs during the time when the policy is paying for your care. This is a wonderful feature.*

Most important, always remember that it isn't the cost of the premiums that will decimate your assets, but the actual cost of paying for the care itself!

Premiums will never impoverish my clients. Care without insurance, on the other hand, could wipe out their assets entirely.

#7 — When I Get Sick I'll Deal with It. Why Should I Worry about It Now?

Here's a sobering reality: Once you need care, you absolutely will not find a company willing to insure you. It is like trying to buy fire insurance while your house is in flames. Once you are sick (and uninsurable), you may ultimately find yourself impoverished: carted off to the kind of nursing home that takes Medicaid patients who are broke!

Waiting until you get sick to deal with it? …It's not even an option.

#8 — I've Got Great Genes; No Strokes or Dementia in My Family.

Count your blessings… but let me tell you about my Aunt Eleanor.

> Eleanor had no family history of heart disease or dementia. In her sixties, she bought a small long term care policy "just in case." She went on with her life in excellent health, continuing to do well until her mid-eighties when she suddenly suffered debilitating fractures in her spine. She had osteoporosis — weak bones — and the pain of her collapsing back was just about more than she could bear.

> Able to walk with a walker, and requiring assistance to get out at all (steps being impossible alone), Eleanor is so grateful for that policy she bought many years ago. "Just in case" has become a necessity.

> By now, Aunt Eleanor has lived a longer, more full life than any of her predecessors. She is the first member of her family to have lived long enough to require the help of caregivers. The fact that there had never been stroke, cardiac arrest, or dementia in her family did not protect her from osteoporosis any more than it could protect her from slipping on winter ice.

Family history is an indicator — but it's not a predictor of your own health!

Remember that not only strokes and dementia trigger the need for care. There are other issues common to older people that make long term care necessary, such as osteoporosis, diabetes, arthritis, Parkinson's disease and emphysema… not to mention drunk drivers, car accidents, and other pitfalls on the road of life.

Obviously, if you take care of yourself, eat right, exercise, and avoid smoking, you have a better chance of remaining healthy for a longer period of time. But it came as a shock to many baseball fans when the late, great Ted Williams suffered a stroke that incapacitated him. If this sports icon could suffer a stroke, where does that leave the rest of us? Just because you've got "great genes" or you "chose the right parents" does not mean that you are immune to long term care issues.

"Just in case" is a whole lot better than "just too late." Just ask Aunt Eleanor.

#9 — We Have Longevity in Our Family — Why Do I Need LTCI?

Good question. You're right — you may not need it for a long, long time. People who live exceptionally long lives often stay healthier longer, too. This doesn't mean you'll never need long-term care, though. It just means that there's a strong possibility that you won't need it as soon as some others might. Of course, familial longevity is only one factor in determining our medical condition as we age.

In any event, let's say you don't need long-term care until you are at an advanced age — say, ninety years old. Then something happens (perhaps a minor stroke) and you need care. Because of your inherent healthiness, you may live for seven more years — requiring some care and physical therapy. This is not an unlikely scenario. What will that care cost you at that time?

> My parents inherited some money at about the time I left for college. It was a true blessing to them. Mother needed care for many years, and my father was able to pay for it.
>
> Dad was in great health until he turned ninety-five. At that point he began to fall, and between the ages of ninety-five and ninety-eight, he managed to use up nearly all his remaining assets for his companion care.

Unfortunately, even people who live to a very ripe old age often do need assistance eventually.

A good long term care insurance plan with built-in inflation on the benefits will be there for you, ready to pay out, even if you are ninety and need to collect until you are ninety-six!

Let's say you're a vigorous, healthy fifty-four now and you don't need care until you turn ninety. If you buy $250 per day in benefits with 5 percent compound inflation, you would receive the following benefits to pay for care beginning at age ninety:

Age	Benefit per Day	Total Benefits per Year
90	$1,379	$503,335
91	1,448	528,520
92	1,520	554,800
93	1,596	582,540
94	1,676	611,740
95	1,760	642,400
96	1,848	674,520

You'll have the care you want when you need it… and decades of peace of mind until then! Not a bad deal.

#10 — Why Should I Buy Now?

Sometimes clients say, "I'll wait until it's closer to when I will need to access coverage, and thereby save money."

If you feel that way, examine the High Cost of Waiting chart in Appendix A.

The reality is that if you wait, you not only need to buy more insurance in the future (due to inflation in the actual cost of care), *but the total cost of policies goes up with your age.*

Of course, if there are changes in your health (which is very likely), this also increases your policy cost. Companies will rate you differently if you have certain physical health problems. Many people in their fifties and sixties may find they have developed osteoporosis or other problems that can add to the cost of premiums.

Therefore, waiting will dramatically add to the total cost of the policy you spend over a lifetime. Of course, the biggest risk is that you will wait too long.

> I have had clients become uninsurable while they were waiting. One couple is now paying the full cost of care themselves, with no help at all from insurance… those three months of indecision about purchasing a policy have cost them thousands and thousands of dollars, to date.

Experts who really understand long term care insurance agree that it does not make sense to wait. They suggest that you buy it in your forties or fifties, if possible. If you are in your forties, you may be still paying your children's tuition and find that getting the full amount of benefits you want will be too much of a strain during those years. If this is the case, you might reasonably consider buying a modest policy to start with ("just in case") and buy the rest in your fifties. On the other hand, if you buy a policy in your late forties, you may be able to afford benefits that will become too expensive later on.

This way some of the benefits will have been purchased at lower rates. Also, if any unexpected problem occurs with your health (for example, a car accident) you will at least have some basic protection. No one who receives money to pay for caregivers is ever sorry for the help they are getting.

According to recent studies reported in *Kiplinger's* magazine,[3] "People who are tapping policies are happy with their coverage. Their main regret [is that] they wish they had bought more."

#11 — Why Should I Pay More to Be Insured by a Top-rated Company?

Everybody loves a bargain.

> Ronny and Celia purchased long term care insurance from a company on the market with rates far below the norm. This

company accepted almost anyone who applied, without checking their health history carefully. They now are insuring a group of policyholders who will need to collect benefits from the company very soon.

Now the company has an underpriced product, and many claimants. The company has turned to the state, saying they don't have enough money to cover the cost of claims, and they need to increase the rates... substantially.

Ronny and Celia are not sure where to turn. They haven't budgeted to allow for such a rise in their premiums, but on the other hand, Celia has some mild hardening of the arteries, and they are both five years older now. They aren't sure that any other company would insure them at a reasonable price anymore.

Two such companies were discussed in the *Wall Street Journal*.[4] (Although the names of the companies appear in the original article, I have removed them from this discussion.)

The insurers erred in the complex business of figuring out how low they can make rates and still have sufficient capital and reserves to pay claims. But instead of taking the full hit themselves, they sought and won premium increases from state regulators. The result is that hundreds of thousands of elderly policyholders are footing the bill for actuarial assumptions that officials at the companies now concede were far too optimistic.

Despite taking riskier business, the two [companies] charged rates that were among the lowest on the market.... Regulators say they didn't spot such red flags because they rarely compare competitors' rates. Instead, regulators rely on statistical assurances from a given insurer that it will be able to pay out a legally mandated percentage of its premium revenues in benefits.

One of these companies began to offer an extremely inexpensive plan. But two years into [this product's] marketing blitz, many of the marginally healthy people [the company] had insured were already sick and seeking reimbursement. Claims were running almost 50 percent higher than forecast, according to [the company's] 1998 filings to state insurance departments. This and other business factors squeezed the company's capital — money on hand for unexpected claims. With the company growing rapidly, its capital relative to the size of its business sank to a level that could trigger a suspension of operations in Florida.

Now, the *Wall Street Journal* was discussing only two companies. There are many excellent, experienced, and honorable companies that price and underwrite in a conservative manner. It bears repeating: *If it looks too good to be true, it probably is.*

It becomes clear that while you may feel it is wise to save money with a cheap product, unhappy people have told me afterward that the cheap policy they originally bought ended up costing as much as — or even more than — the policy from the better company after only a few years. They have already had several increases and fear more of the same. With a fine conservative company, they would have had stable rates and not feared that the company might go out of business altogether.

Why, you may ask, do agents sell these cheap plans? There are several reasons:

- With cheap rates it is easier to close the sale and beat out the competition.
- The commissions these companies offer agents are very high.
- A company that is aggressively pushing its product treats its brokers to extras. It handles its agents with kid gloves, knowing that a small investment in broker incentives reaps great rewards in policies sold!

Agents need backbone, *and need to consider the client's future first.* You may have noticed that I call my clients "clients" and not "customers" or "sales." I have been in business since 1982 and have always wanted to be able to face my clients with pride. I will lose a commission rather than sell a product that is not in my client's best interests.

That's what it takes to be a good broker… *and that is why I wrote this book: to give you all the information you need to make the best decision that is right for you.*

If it looks too good to be true…
If it looks too cheap…
If the contract offers too much…
If the company is too small…
If the ratings are poor…
Watch out!

How can you pick a reliable insurance company?

Make sure you see all the ratings that are meaningful. See what the major reviewers (AM Best, Moody's, Fitch, Standard and Poor's, and Weiss) say about a company. Make sure the insurer you're considering has sold long term care insurance for at least ten years.

There are plenty of legitimate companies out there. Consider companies that have had no rate increases on in-force business to date. If a company says they are "number one," ask, "What are you number one in?" Alphabetical order? Or paying claims in a timely fashion?

An occasional moderate rate increase may be acceptable under certain circumstances. For example, the first company in the long term care insurance business was a real pioneer. They have had to raise premiums because early on there was no claims-and-utilization experience to draw upon. Also, they have been called upon to add features to their old contracts, which can be costly. (An example of this is adding an assisted living benefit to a nursing home contract.)

Also — and this may shock you — don't go by recommendations from a leading consumer magazine. They actually have more than once selected as their best recommendations companies that have gone out of business shortly thereafter — once, even by the time the issue was on the newsstands! It may be that they rate by price alone and don't consider underwriting factors.

Finally — do not be afraid to buy long term care coverage just because there are some irresponsible companies working in this field. Do your homework and make sure you are going with a highly respected, highly rated company with at least ten years of experience in this area of insurance.

Ultimately, this policy will be one of the most valuable items you have ever purchased!

#12 — Why Does Underwriting Take So Long?

The underwriting process is not difficult, yet it can take a long time to get your answer. This is because of the time it takes to get copies of your medical records. It is especially time consuming when certain HMOs are involved, where getting the records can take as long as two months.

Be sure to request on your application that the age at which you are applying be the age they will use for your pricing. This will alleviate the strain of a long wait for records.

⌒

Many people find it helpful to set a time frame, perhaps three or four weeks in which they research the insurance policies, and then apply. I have seen people let the process drag on so long that they forget all they have heard and thought about, get overwhelmed, and give up. Most frustrating is when clients spend so long considering the issue that a critical birthday passes, and they suddenly discover, to their dismay, that the same policy will now cost them more.

For your own sake, once you start to really examine LTCI, it is important to maintain momentum. *Consider the information, and interview brokers until you find one who is knowledgeable and whom you trust. Then make a decision and apply.*

CHAPTER 7

Your Complete Guide to Long Term Care Insurance

What is Long Term Care Insurance?

Long term care insurance (LTCI) pays for care in nursing homes, residential care facilities, or for home care. Nurses, therapists, home health aides, and other skilled and unskilled caregivers provide long term care that is covered under LTCI.

LTCI pays for the cost of care after injury or illness, when an individual cannot perform two or more activities of daily living without substantial help from another person. *Activities of daily living* are defined as:

- bathing
- dressing
- eating (the ability to feed oneself)
- transferring (moving in and out of bed, a chair, or wheelchair, or getting around the home)
- getting to and from the toilet, and other aspects of personal hygiene
- continence (the ability to maintain bowel and bladder control)

LTCI also covers severe cognitive loss (for example, Alzheimer's). Cognitive loss alone will qualify you to receive benefits.

LTCI does *not* cover the services provided by doctors, surgeons, chiropractors, or others whose services are normally provided by regular medical insurance; it does not provide coverage in a hospital setting. Nor is it the same thing as disability insurance, which provides for the continuation of income should one become disabled in the course of one's career (LTCI does not replace income).

Usually, when a person suffers a major injury, a stroke, Parkinson's, severe arthritis, or develops dementia such as Alzheimer's disease, he or she qualifies to collect on long term insurance, even if the injury or illness will heal with time.

What Benefits Are Covered by LTCI Policies?

All LTCI policies are not created equal. You'll want to discuss with your insurance broker the various options that make the most sense for you. *There is no "One Size Fits All" when it comes to LTCI.*

There is enormous variety in the number and type of plans available. Most LTCI plans are comprehensive and cover home care, nursing home care, and care in assisted living facilities. However, there are policies that pay only for care in a facility, and there are some that pay only for care at home.

LTCI policies can cover some or all of the following benefits:

- skilled nursing care and home health aides in your home
- care or assistance with daily activities in your home
- homemaker, companion, personal care attendant, or chore services, including meal preparation, housework, grooming and dressing assistance, medication dispensing, and shopping
- occupational therapy, physical therapy, respiratory therapy, speech therapy, and medical social workers
- hospice care in one's home
- adult day care (community-based facilities that allow your family caregiver to work or conduct business during the day, while allowing you to enjoy the comforts of home at night)
- home modifications, such as grab bars in the tub or shower, guardrails on the front porch, widening doorways, lowering light switches, etc.

- therapeutic services such as hospital-style beds, etc.
- medical alert systems

In addition, some LTCI contracts even provide benefits to family caregivers:

- Informal caregivers in your home (such as your spouse or child) may be reimbursed for training in how to provide the kind of care required.

- A "Respite Care Benefit" pays so that a family member caring for the individual can get away for a vacation or an emergency.

LTCI Benefits

Typically, all pre-existing conditions are covered immediately once the LTCI policy is approved. There is no waiting period for specific health conditions.

A good LTCI policy covers the same broad spectrum of benefits whether you are at home, in a nursing home, or in an assisted living facility. Generally, you cannot choose a member of your immediate family to be the paid caregiver under LTCI. Some policies, however, offer this feature for an additional cost.

Since LTCI does not pay for hospital care, some people wonder what might happen if they have to leave a nursing home or residential care facility for a few weeks to go to the hospital for tests, or for care of an acute infection. LTCI policies will usually pay twenty to fifty days per calendar year for the cost of saving your bed in a nursing home or assisted living facility so that you do not lose your place while you are hospitalized.

If you need long term care temporarily and then you become well again, you can still receive benefits under the same policy if necessary, provided that the benefits were not depleted during the course of the first illness.

The "Elimination Period" — a Vital Aspect of LTCI

LTCI contracts contain something called an *elimination period*. The elimination period is the number of days between the beginning of the need for help with activities of daily living or the onset of serious dementia, and the date the payments under the policy begin (say, thirty days later).

You can choose an elimination period anywhere from zero days up to a year. Preferably, choose an elimination period of no longer than ninety days, because it is possible to rack up serious home health care bills even in just a ninety-day period. Even thirty days hits the pocketbook hard!

The longer the elimination period, the lower the cost of the policy. If you buy at a younger age, the cost difference in the policy is very small, in which case it is certainly worthwhile to get a short elimination period.

In general, the more inclusive the policy, the more it will cost. You may need to compare prices on several different combinations of benefits to find one that fits both your lifestyle preferences and your wallet.

LTCI Benefits and Your Taxes

Most new LTCI policies are *tax qualified.* This means that the IRS has given a binding opinion stating that benefits under the policy will never be taxed.

If you choose a *nontax-qualified* LTCI policy, you run some risk of seeing your benefits taxed in later years. Premiums on nontax-qualified LTCI plans are never deductible. (For tax-qualified plans, the answer may be yes — consult with your tax adviser.)

However, some features of nontax-qualified plans may be extremely financially beneficial for you and your family. At this time, everyone receiving benefits gets a form 1099. The question of whether to purchase a tax-qualified or nontax-qualified policy is a subject to discuss with both your tax accountant and insurance broker.

Worldwide Coverage

LTCI can offer a special advantage to those who wish to retire overseas. While some policies only cover individuals residing in the United States, other policies offer coverage for those who want to retire to a villa in Tuscany, an apartment in Jerusalem, or in other parts of the world.

Be sure to ask your broker for this feature if there is even the slightest chance that you will wish to move abroad someday. Never just assume that your policy is good worldwide.

> Anna comes from a large but close-knit family. Her brothers
> and cousins all live in Rome. Although already somewhat frail,
> she plans to move near her family sometime in the next few
> years, and hire part-time caregivers as needed in Italy… funded
> by her LTCI policy.

If you are told the policy will cover you worldwide, make sure it says so in the policy contract. Otherwise, you may request a letter from the company confirming this feature, which you should keep together with your policy contract.

Premiums — and How to Protect Them

Insurance companies are prohibited from singling people out and increasing their premiums. State governments must approve any increases — and those increases would affect an entire state and policy class. This means that a company cannot just tell you that you have to pay more for your policy; they have to change the prices for everybody on the plan.

It is possible that rates will go up someday. Some people choose to pay off their entire LTCI policy premiums in ten years to avoid worrying about rate increases later. *When you buy from a top company that prices fairly and underwrites carefully, you will probably not see a significant rate increase for many years.*

The bottom line? Choose an insurer with high ratings and at least ten years of experience in the long term care field. If that insurer does not have a history of large rate increases, prices fairly, and does its due diligence in underwriting, you can feel fairly secure that the rates you pay for your policy will be stable for a long time. If rates are increased, you can lower the benefits, if necessary, to bring down your costs.

Most policies offer a discount of 10 to 25 percent when both spouses purchase LTCI.

Protecting Your Benefits against Inflation

Most LTCI policies offer an *inflation rider,* which means that the benefits rise each year in accordance with a specified figure in the policy.

Take the inflation rider, because the costs of care will continue to rise. The insurance rider makes sure that the benefit level you choose today will not be severely devalued by inflation by the time you actually need the benefits. Some companies call the inflation rider the *Automatic Increase Benefit* or AIB.

You can choose *simple interest* or *compound interest.* For example, say you choose a policy with a $200 daily benefit, and only need to draw benefits on that policy after twenty years. With simple interest added on for those twenty years, the payout would actually be $400 a day. With compound interest, that $200 daily benefit would rise to $505 per day. (See Appendix B for more details.)

If you are under seventy years of age, you should purchase a policy with 5 percent compound inflation. If you are seventy or over, you can choose 5 percent with simple inflation. The actual level of inflation in long term care costs is approximately 6 percent, but most companies offer a 5 percent inflation rider. No policy should be sold without an inflation rider, unless a person is well into his eighties, and just can't afford the rider. Avoid plan options (often called COLI or Future Purchase Options) which allow you to defer purchasing inflation increases until later, because you will ultimately spend more by purchasing inflation at older ages.

The "Pool of Money"

Long term care insurance, like all forms of insurance, can be purchased in varying amounts. You choose the level of benefits when you choose a policy.

Most policies provide *expense reimbursement benefits* in accordance with the receipts you provide from your health providers, up to the limit of the policy. Under some policies, *indemnity benefits* are provided, and you actually receive the amount of money per day that your policy indicates, even if you wish to use a portion of the money for noncovered benefits, such as care management.

To illustrate the *pool of money,* let us say your benefit level provides for $200 a day worth of services, but you use only $150 a day:

- Under expense reimbursement policies with *unlimited lifetime benefits,* you continue to collect your benefits for as many years as you need them, but you do forfeit the use of money you do not spend on any particular day (in this case, $50 a day).

- On policies with a *limited payout period* (say, two to ten years), when you reach the end of the time period, that "leftover" $50 per day would remain in what insurers call your *pool of money.* You can continue to collect those benefits that you didn't spend until you drain the pool of money. (You can calculate the pool of money by multiplying the number of days in the benefit period you select by the maximum daily benefit.)

Comparing Daily, Weekly, and Monthly Benefits

- *Daily benefits:* If you have a six-year benefit period that pays a $200 daily benefit, you are entitled to 365 benefit days multiplied by six years (365 x 6). That's 2,190 days of benefits, multiplied by the $200 maximum daily benefit under your policy, and you come up with a *maximum policy benefit* of $438,000 (plus inflation).

  When benefits are calculated on a daily basis, if on any given day you spent only $150 of your $200 maximum daily benefit, the remaining $50 "left over" is either forfeited or returned to the pool of money for use after your benefit period ends.

Many companies offer a weekly or monthly benefit. With a little simple math (a calculator helps!), you can compare the benefits:

- *Weekly benefits:* In a weekly benefit, you can combine all the leftover benefits from the days of that week into one lump sum to use. Suppose you have $200 a day and a weekly benefit. You have $1,400 a week to spend. If you spent $150 a day for a live-in caregiver, you would have spent $1,050 each week, and would have $350 left over each week. You might use that $350 for physical therapy or other special help you need that is covered by your contract. (With a daily benefit you would have had several $50 leftovers, none of which on their own would be enough to pay the physical therapist for a visit.)

- *Monthly benefits:* If the benefits are calculated monthly, you would have $200 times a thirty-day month, or $6,000 per month available. This gives you a lot of flexibility in using the money to your best advantage.

Certification

Certification is required only for tax-qualified policies. When the government gave its stamp of approval to tax-qualified long term care insurance plans, it wanted to make sure that the care to be provided really was *long term.* So the government set a requirement of ninety days of need, and requires certification.

If you have a tax-qualified plan, and you require assistance, you will need to get certification from a health care practitioner that you need care for at least ninety days in order to start collecting under your long term care insurance policy. *Until you get that certification, however, insurance companies are not permitted by law to pay during the first ninety days on tax-qualified plans* — even if your elimination period is shorter than ninety days.

If a person is diagnosed with dementia or Parkinson's, or suffers a serious stroke, their doctor will almost certainly immediately certify that care will be needed for more than ninety days. I have had clients receive ninety-day certifications for broken bones that are expected to mend slowly.

⌒

When a person needs help with either physical or mental activities due to injury, illness, or cognitive loss, LTCI benefits provide for a wide variety of services at home, in a nursing home, or in an assisted-living facility. With a well-designed policy, you or a person you have designated can choose where you live, what care you will receive, and who will care for you.

Variables to Consider When You Sit Down
to Compare Long Term Care Insurance Policies

- **How much money do you want to receive per day under the policy?**

- **Does the company offer a specific amount of money for a nursing home, but less for at-home care?** *Make sure you get 100 percent of the nursing home benefits at home...* anything else will defeat getting the care you need at home! Neglecting to insist on full benefits for home care is one of the biggest mistakes LTCI purchasers make.

- **Will the policy pay for your long term care expenses on a daily, weekly or monthly basis?** Try to get a monthly benefit, since it gives you the most flexibility; weekly is next best.

  All things being equal, opt against a daily benefit (usually found in older policies), which restricts how you can benefit from the policy. One study showed that individuals incur lower expenses on some days and relatively higher expenses on other days. For accommodating real-life schedules, policies with weekly or monthly benefit budgets are best. (One new policy calculates benefits based on a 31-day month, rather than the standard 30-day month. This adds up to 372 days of benefits per year!)

- **What is the minimum benefit period — that is, how many years would you like the policy to cover you?** This can be anywhere from one year to unlimited coverage. A "five-year plan" means five years' worth of benefits will be available to you whenever you need it. If you buy a plan at age fifty-four and begin to collect at age eighty-five, you will be able to collect for five years or until the pool of money is drained.

- **How long an elimination period do you want?** A policy can offer a choice of zero days, 30 days, 60 days, 90 days, 180 days, or 365 days. *I recommend taking as short an elimination period as you can afford.*

- **Do you want an inflation rider, where the value of your benefits gradually increases to lessen the impact of inflation?** Do you want the benefits to increase by 5 percent *compound* interest, or 5 percent *simple* interest? You almost certainly want some type of inflation rider, unless you are already in your mid-eighties. *I don't recommend using the cost of living index that some companies offer, because each time you buy more LTCI, you pay for the added benefits at the rate corresponding to your new (older) age.*

- **Do you qualify for a marital discount?** Are you and your spouse both purchasing long term care insurance at the same time? If you are, an additional discount might be available to you, generally 10 to 25 percent.

- **Do you want a tax-qualified or nontax-qualified plan?** Most top companies now offer tax-qualified plans exclusively.

- **Do you want international coverage?** For what country(ies)?

- **Do you prefer a plan with a care management requirement, or do you prefer to select someone to do this for you?**

- **Do you prefer expense reimbursement or an indemnity plan?** An indemnity plan pays the full daily benefit even if you do not spend the full amount.

- **How often would you like to receive your billing statement:** on an annual, semiannual, quarterly, or monthly basis?

Find a Broker You Can Trust to Keep Your Best Interests at the Forefront

It can be hard — even overwhelming — trying to make sense of these decisions on one's own. I never recommend that anyone seek to avoid a broker's commission by buying LTCI over the Internet — the commission will have to be paid anyway, and all that is bypassed is a broker's experienced personal advice.

Find a broker you can trust, and feel free to ask the questions that we discuss in this book. Don't feel obligated to buy a particular policy just because it's your broker's "special of the month." Your physical well-being, emotional security, and financial security — and that of your family — will be protected by this policy… it needs to be right for *you*. A professional LTCI specialist can advise and guide you.

It is important to realize that the plans available to you will depend on your health and age — you may be limited in terms of the companies to which you can apply, especially if you've procrastinated for a while, and missed a "cutoff" age. Just as you select clothing you buy to fit your size, you need to have a broker find companies that are willing to insure your particular health history… and then choose from those top companies available to you.

One of the best questions you can ask your broker, financial planner, accountant, or attorney is just what sort of plan they have for themselves! Professionals who have taken the time to study these issues for themselves are likely to do a much better job for you — because they've sat where you are sitting. (Of course, this doesn't mean that the same plan is right for you. It just means that your adviser has done his or her homework.)

Congratulations! You are well prepared now to steer your way through the myriad details in LTCI. You are a well-educated LTCI consumer.

STEP TWO:

Geriatric Care Management

CHAPTER 8

Take Good Care of Yourself

Your family will not stop loving you if you fall ill, any more than you would stop loving them if they got sick. Your spouse and children will want to help you recuperate, and to feel comfortable again. What you need to consider is how helping you over a long period — months, or even years — may affect the ones you love most.

"In Sickness and in Health…"

The mental and emotional strain of caregiving results in a substantially higher risk of mortality to an elderly spouse. *In other words, it could kill your spouse to take care of you.*

This is not a scare tactic, but information from a study cited in the *Journal of the American Medical Association*.[5] This study showed that spousal caregivers age 66 to 96 who are under strain, and are living with and caring for a sick spouse, *have a 63 percent higher risk of mortality than they would otherwise.*

> Our study suggests that being a caregiver who is experiencing mental or emotional strain is an independent risk for mortality among elderly spousal caregivers. Caregivers who report strain associated with caregiving are more likely to die than noncaregiving [spouses].

> Although family caregivers perform an important service for

society and their relatives, they do so at considerable cost to themselves. There is strong consensus that caring for an elderly individual with a disability is burdensome and stressful to many family members and contributes to psychiatric morbidity in the form of increased depression.

This study also reported that caregivers have reduced immunity to disease, and are more prone to illnesses. They have more cardiovascular problems, and they experience slower wound healing. They are much less likely to get enough rest when they are healthy, take time to rest when they are sick, or have time to exercise and take care of their own health.

Caregivers who provide support to their spouse and report caregiving strain are far more likely to die within four years than noncaregivers. They have significantly higher levels of depression, anxiety, and poor health.

I'm not suggesting that a healthy spouse should not play a role in the treatment of an ailing spouse. But why not shift the burden of the work and the cost of long term care from your spouse to professional caregivers? *Plan to stay home with paid caregivers, and don't put that burden on your husband or wife.*

"My Kids Will Take Care of Me"

You have wonderful, devoted children. They really want to care for you if you ever need help. But are they working? Would they have the time to meet your need for care? And how old will they be when you require their help?

A recent study[6] sought to determine the total financial and personal costs of caregiving to workers. *Nearly two-thirds of respondents reported that caregiving had a direct impact on their earnings.* Total loss in wage wealth was substantial, with an average loss of $566,443. (Wage wealth is the present value of lifetime wages calculated as of the date of retirement.) As well as current income, caregivers' retirement savings suffered and pension benefits fell.

Adding together the lost wages, social security, and pension benefits, the average total loss was $659,139 over an average lifetime.

"We call it the caregiver's glass ceiling," said Sandra

Timmermann, a gerontologist and director of the MetLife
Mature Market Institute. "It's an issue that will become even
more critical within the next five to ten years."

What does this mean to you? It means that it could cost your son or daughter two-thirds of a million dollars, not to mention their marriage or even their sanity, just to take care of you.

Today, 31 percent of family caregivers quit work to care for an older person. Nearly two-thirds cut back on their work schedule, more than a quarter take a leave of absence, and 10 percent turn down promotions because of their caregiving responsibilities. It costs the typical working caregiver about $109 dollars a day in lost wages and health benefits to provide full-term care at home... very nearly approaching the cost of paid caregivers.

You also risk a child's resentment.

A fifty-three-year-old developmental psychologist reported that
she nursed her eighty-year-old mother through end-stage kidney
cancer. Providing twenty-four-hour care in her home for her
mother was far more taxing than she had ever imagined. "I felt
completely overwhelmed," she said. "Why did she do this to me?"

The *New York Times* reported on a survey that depicted the true face of elder care.[7] Of nearly 1,500 people over 65 who were surveyed, 29 percent said they relied on a daughter or daughter-in-law for care, while 12 percent said they relied on a son.

You may not need long term care until you are in your eighties or even nineties. How old will your children be then? In their sixties and seventies? Taking care of *your* health needs could very well exacerbate *theirs*. Wouldn't it be much more responsible and loving to handle your long term care needs yourself?

Your child will need to give up time with her own spouse, children, and grand-children because of the need to care for you. The exhaustion, depression, and depletion of your child will erode her health and quality of life. Is it really fair to put the children you love under such a burden?

I think not.

CHAPTER 9

Geriatric Care Managers — a Most Valuable Resource

The expectation that prevails in virtually every ethnic group in our society is that a loved one will have to put her own life on hold to care for an infirm parent.

Now, I am not suggesting an abdication of responsibility on the part of children. There is already far too much of that in society. I *am* saying that there are certain limits to what should be expected of relatives. It absolutely behooves you to choose a primary caregiver who is not related to you.

A *geriatric care manager* (GCM) — a professional who specializes in assisting older people and their families with long term care arrangements — may be the most valuable resource you have in planning your long term care. GCMs have training in gerontology, social work, nursing, or counseling. Their job is to help you in the following ways:

- Identify obstacles, and eligibility and need for services

- Screen, arrange, and monitor in-home help or other services

- Review financial, legal, and medical issues and offer referrals to geriatric specialists to anticipate problems and conserve assets

- Act as a liaison to families at a distance, making sure things are going well and alerting families to problems

- Provide consumer education and advocacy

- Assist with moving an older person to or from a retirement complex, care home, or nursing home

A geriatric care manager will visit the individual at home, ask about his or her life, note any difficulties or problems, check the house for possible safety hazards, and meet with other family members. Based on these assessments, the GCM will make recommendations: Perhaps someone should come in several times a week to help with cooking, cleaning, and bathing; perhaps some form of therapy (speech, physical, occupational) would be helpful; perhaps some changes would make the home easier to navigate.

A GCM can also be hired to help in a crisis, or even to prevent one. Prior to a vacation, a care manager can meet with you and your parent, and note information about your parent's medical insurance, doctors, and so forth. The care manager can check on your parent and be there to help if needed.

> Naomi and Milt hired a GCM while Milt's mother was recovering from pacemaker implantation surgery. They enjoyed a much-needed vacation out of state, knowing that she was taken care of, and that someone would contact them in case of need.

There may be many resources all around of which you are not aware. A geriatric care manager who knows the area in which your parent or parents live may save you tens, or even hundreds, of hours of research and phone calls. GCMs have extensive knowledge about the cost, quality, and availability of services in their community. A GCM can connect you with the services an older person may need.

Some GCMs also provide family or individual counseling, support, money management, and conservatorship or guardianship assistance.

A Geriatric Care Manager's Success Story
by Judith Tobenkin, MS, MSG, Certified Care Manager

> Stan enjoyed a successful career as a consultant to industrial businesses and retired from his work around 1980 with $1.3 million in savings and investments. Stan has no family at all, a situation

that is not altogether unusual in today's world. After doing some research, Stan decided to hire a geriatric care manager in the mid-1980s, because he feared he might someday need care and he wanted to be sure that he would be cared for at home.

We spoke and visited occasionally throughout the five years that Stan was still actively driving his car and managing his business affairs. He explained to me his preferences with regard to food, music, activities, lifestyle, and so on. In the early 1990s, Stan's mental and physical condition began to deteriorate. Stan's firm desires to remain at home were communicated frequently and clearly both to me and to his accountant, Wanda Schenk.

As his illnesses progressed, Stan's at-home needs increased. Slowly, the payroll for his in-home help has grown to the point where he currently spends $70,000 a year on care. This includes salaries, payroll taxes, food, utilities, insurance, and so on. He requires round-the-clock care (two twelve-hour shifts) seven days a week, because he can no longer be left alone.

Obviously this is a bittersweet story. However, Stan planned ahead! I know him, and I know his personal wishes about most aspects of living. I make sure that Stan remains at home, where he earnestly desires to be. Wanda and I oversee physical improvements to Stan's home designed to improve his safety there: installation of pleasant, sturdy carpet to facilitate the use of a walker and then a wheelchair; various bathroom safety devices; and the repair and installation of better electrical systems.

Wanda Schenk, Stan's CPA, has been an integral partner of his caregiving team. She and I are Stan's co-trustees. Wanda has worked with Stan's broker to oversee a gradual shift in his investments from securities and mutual funds to more conservative assets such as municipal bonds, Treasury notes, and other vehicles which provide a greater level of principal preservation and steady income flow.

Wanda provides bookkeeping services twice a month to handle the payroll, pay bills, and do filing. It is my responsibility to supervise the hiring and day-to-day services of the in-home care-givers and to coordinate health services as necessary. Wanda and I also make separate visits once a month to make sure that Stan is getting the best possible care and that everything is going smoothly.

We each review the caregivers' notes, check the entire apartment for cleanliness, ensure that there is an adequate food supply that is being stored correctly, review Stan's diet and eating habits, com-municate with medical personnel, and spend time just visiting with Stan. We then report our observations to one another.

I am more involved with Stan's health care needs, and Wanda is more involved with the financial aspects of his life. Yet, we both work together in all areas to ensure that Stan is always well cared for. Working together as a team, Wanda and I continue to try to provide the highest quality of life possible for Stan, whom we've come to love and cherish.

Consider for a moment what Stan's life would have been like had he not planned ahead. He would have been removed from his own home. He would have become an institutionalized human being, a statistic, and probably would have died years ago. He would have been robbed of his dignity. Geriatric care manage-ment has quite literally changed his life.

CHAPTER 10

Hiring Caregivers

Sometimes, just the idea of hiring caregivers to work in the home can be completely overwhelming. Most people do not have previous experience in searching for and hiring employees, and don't have any idea where to begin. Anne Hanssen has a master's degree in gerontology, and is the director of Gerontology Home Companion, a home care aide organization located in Woodland Hills, California. She offers this advice about hiring caregivers:

> There are several options when choosing someone to help you care for a family member. For many, a full-service agency is the best choice. The agency provides payroll, bonding, insurance and supervision of employees, for a higher hourly or daily rate.
>
> If cost of care is a factor, a placement agency or private-hire attendant are good alternatives. To hire an attendant privately, many families are successful in finding people through friends who have trusted caregivers or through referral lists from senior centers, family service agencies and other resources that serve the disabled community.
>
> Although the services of a home care aide are not usually covered by health insurance, many long term care insurance policies do cover attendant care at home and are very flexible about how a family chooses to hire an aide.

Manuals and guides for hiring caregivers have long lists of questions to ask an attendant or an agency. Our organization uses the following guidelines to select caring, effective caregivers:

References: I know of agencies that tout fingerprinting and police background checks, but fail to call the persons for whom the aide worked previously. If a candidate can provide no references, move on. Even if a previous employer has died, there is almost always a family member, friend, or physician who is happy to provide a reference for a good caregiver. If an aide worked in a hospital where the personnel office provides only dates of employment, there is usually a supervisor or nurse who is willing to help an excellent coworker. *Insist on references!*

Experience: Some aides prefer work that involves some medical care; some are excellent with people who are confined to bed. Some aides love helping with rehabilitation and assisting a client's return to participation in household and community activities; others do a great job with people with dementia. Some aides seem good with almost everyone! Look carefully at your own situation and choose someone you think would blend well with your care and household requirements. Give this more consideration than how trim and tidy the aide looks in her uniform.

Training: I have yet to meet an aide who is not interested in receiving more information and training. Many states have certificates for aides who have completed a specified number of hours of classroom and hands-on experience. Be aware that the quality of these programs is uneven at best, and that even aides who have taken a training program and have a certificate may not have good judgment or common sense. Determine how important a certificate is for your needs. Keep in mind that some aides may work long hours and have demanding family responsibilities that have made classroom participation difficult for them, but they may be excellent aides with extraordinary skills they have learned *on the job*, perhaps trained by physicians, therapists, nurses, and families. Participation in training programs is important, but it is only one component to consider when hiring an attendant.

Live-in or live-out? A live-in assignment is appropriate when the person needing care does not need constant attention and sleeps reasonably well at night.

Many aides choose to live in because transportation is difficult for them. A live-in aide who drives is rare indeed. Realistically evaluate your need for a live-in aide. If you are sure you need someone to live in and you can manage without someone who drives, your pool of candidates will increase greatly. Many aides and the people they care for are able to use a taxi or transport service to do marketing, errands, and other appointments.

An important tip when hiring a live-in aide: Make sure the caregiver will be able to sleep reasonably well at night. Although we can all have a rough or rocky night occasionally, and need extra support, repeated short and interrupted periods of sleep will result in a tired and cranky caregiver whose mood and judgment will become impaired.

On behalf of caregivers, part-time or full-time: Most caregivers need to work full-time. It is with this job that they pay rent and feed their families. If your need is for part-time assistance, understand that an assignment with you will probably be paired with one or more assignments with other families. For example, an aide would probably be happy with four hours each morning or four hours in the afternoon. It is unlikely that someone will stay with an assignment that requires a few hours Monday morning, Thursday afternoon, and Sunday morning.

Almost no one wants to work every weekend. Like everyone else, aides have families, religious observances, and special occasions to attend. Those who do work weekends probably also work during the week. If you are flexible and understanding, aides appreciate your attitude, and go out of their way to help.

A "caregiver heart": Over the years we've met some extraordinary men and women who work with older clients at home *because they love to.* When you are considering candidates, look for someone who would *love* to care for you or your family member.

Listen to how they describe their last job, and the one before that. Make sure that your candidate wants to stay on the job for a while, not just until the computer programming class is available. Your instinct will probably be saying something; listen to it! Look for an aide with a caregiver heart!

Karen Shoff's Suggested Caregiver Interview Sheet

On the next two pages you will find the forms I used when I myself was interviewing caregivers for my father. I found it useful to attach instant snapshots (Polaroids) of the candidates (which I took at the first interview) to help me remember with whom I spoke. You might ask applicants to bring along their own picture, if you think it's easier.

Check references! You'd be shocked at the ways people can stretch the truth! You are bringing people into your home to care for someone you love; it's worth making a few phone calls to be sure you're getting a caregiver you can trust.

Karen Shoff's
CAREGIVER INTERVIEW SHEET℠

Date: _____

Name: _____

Phone: (day) _____

(evening) _____

Address: _____

_____

_____

**(Attach photo
of applicant here)**

Source of this referral: _____

Married: ❑ Yes ❑ No   Smoker: ❑ Yes ❑ No

Children: ❑ Yes #_____ ❑ No   Licensed to drive: ❑ Yes ❑ No

Do you prefer to ❑ live in? ❑ or out?   Owns a car: ❑ Yes ❑ No

Work schedule:

Day: ❑ Yes ❑ No   Preferred hours: _____

Night: ❑ Yes ❑ No   Preferred hours: _____

What days are you available? _____

Work Experience

	Name:	Phone:	Nature of Position:
1.			
2.			
3.			
4.			

References

	Name:	Phone:	How You Know Them:
1.			
2.			
3.			
4.			

Questions to Ask a Potential Caregiver:

What type of jobs have you enjoyed the most?

What aspects of your work do you like best, and find most interesting and/or rewarding?

Tell me about your favorite jobs.

Tell me about people you have cared for before.

If you could have a perfect job, what would it be?

What do you feel are your strengths?

What are your weaknesses?

Note your instinctive feelings about the candidate.

Questions to Ask References:

How do you know the applicant?

When and for how long did you employ him/her?

What was the nature of the work duties?

How did he/she handle the duties?

Do you believe this applicant to be…

    …honest?   …hard working?

    …prompt/on time?   …reliable?

    …organized and orderly?

What are the strengths of the applicant (things they are best at)?

What areas need work (weaker areas)?

Would you hire this person again?

Any advice and suggestions you have, or any other comments?

Note how enthusiastic the reference seemed to be.

Is Your Home Ready for You?

Could you live comfortably in your home if you were in a wheelchair? Another important consideration in your planning is the suitability of your home. Visualize adjustments that give you easy access to the bathroom from your bedroom, and direct access to the outside. (Some long term care insurance policies will pay for home modifications once you have an active claim.)

Consider this excerpt from *Modern Maturity*[8]:

> And then there was the moment in the laundry room when we were about to enter the downstairs bathroom (a full bath, luckily for us). Rosemary stopped me and invited me to consider whether I could make that turn if I were in a wheelchair. "You would need thirty-six inches across," she said, and in my mind's eye I was 36 inches wide....
>
> "The space between the sink and the tub is too narrow to enable me to wheel through to the toilet." I imagined myself wheeling through to the toilet. "You'll need some handholds here," she said. I imagined myself lifting my body out of the wheelchair and onto the toilet.

Can your home be made suitable, or do you need to consider a move to a place that will be appropriate for you in your later years?

If you are considering moving at any time, look for a home that will accommodate long term needs. Find a house with no steps to the entrance or between rooms, and where the bedroom and bathroom are on the main floor, requiring no use of stairs. Try to have an extra bedroom or den available for a caregiver to sleep in.

> After her husband's death, Margaret felt very lonely. She didn't like rattling around their sprawling, ten-room house, so she sold it and bought a stylish three-level condominium.
>
> A year later, Margaret was diagnosed with breast cancer. The treatments left her physically spent, and she found herself sleeping on the living room couch, unable to muster the strength

to climb the stairs to her bedroom. Two months later, frustrated beyond belief, Margaret moved to an assisted-living facility. She is reasonably happy there, but misses the privacy and independence of having her own home.

Thinking ahead is what good planning is all about.

CHAPTER 11

More about Geriatric Care Management

by Steven Barlam, MSW, LCSW, Geriatric Care Manager

As a care manager who has been in practice since 1985, I have worked with many families who are looking for solutions to their eldercare needs. There are common themes that have emerged illustrating the value of what care management has to offer families. Through the actual scenarios that follow, you will find how families have gotten relief by using professional care management services.

For Out-of-Town Family Members Who Could Benefit from a Local Professional to Provide Supervision, Feedback, and Support

Jenny lives in Ohio and is happily married with two adolescent sons in high school. Her mother, Sally, lives in California. Since her mother's recent stroke, Jenny feels particularly responsible for ensuring that her mother's needs are met. She speaks to her mother regularly, but somehow she never really feels convinced that everything is going as well as her mother reports. She remembers when her mother fell and didn't tell her for two weeks. She finds that she is spending a lot of time worrying about her mother, and wishes that she could live closer.

The geriatric care manager working with Jenny reaches out to her mother. Through the trusting relationship that is developed,

Sally allows the geriatric care manager to make semiregular visits to check in with her. Sally enjoys speaking with the GCM, since it allows her the opportunity to connect in a meaningful way with someone who is compassionate and understanding. The care manager, with Sally's permission, maintains contact with Jenny. The care manager is able to make suggestions over time that Sally makes use of to improve her quality of life.

For Those Who Want to Do the Right Thing and Are Just Not Sure What That Is

Mark is a very involved son. He cares a great deal about his parents, and has noticed that his mother's memory has deteriorated recently. His father is doing his best to help out; however, Mark notices that his father is becoming rather frazzled, losing patience, and not taking care of business as he always had.

Mark wants to step in and help his parents. He is willing to take them into his own home, or find them an assisted living facility or even arrange for care in their own home — but he's just not sure what would be the best solution for his parents. His father is so overwhelmed that it is hard for Mark to know how to involve him in these important decisions.

Mark engages the services of a geriatric care manager to help him evaluate the situation. The GCM meets with Mark and his parents, talks with his mother's doctor, and finds out what is important to all involved. The GCM suggests a thorough medical evaluation for the mother, and that in the short term the father hire someone for a limited number of hours each week to allow him to take a break. After analyzing the information obtained, the geriatric care manager offers suggestions that are tailor-made to the whole family's needs.

For Families in Which the Siblings and/or the Parent(s) Can't See Eye to Eye on What to Do in Response to the Parent's Needs

Robert is tired of getting those frantic calls from his parents asking him to go to the market and pick up a few things for them. He offers to go to the market once a week, but he finds that they are not able to plan ahead and always need something mid-week requiring him to "drop everything" and get the crucial item to them ASAP. In his frustration he has investigated an assisted living facility that has a market next door. Robert's out-of-town sisters, Louise and Pat, vehemently disagree with their brother about moving their parents, and are in favor of hiring an in-home caregiver who drives. Their parents are opposed to moving and to accepting any in-home care, since they feel they are managing just fine.

Following an assessment visit, the geriatric care manager facilitates a conference call with all involved. During the call, all parties articulated their desires, and the GCM crafted a recommendation that attended to everyone's needs. In this situation it is clear that the parents do not want to accept care because it symbolizes that they cannot take care of business in the manner they once did.

Presenting encapsulated care, namely, hiring someone to do errands once a week and framing it in terms of *meeting the son's needs* as opposed to the *parents needing care* made it easier for the parents to accept.

An additional underlying issue for the parents was the fear that if they had someone else running the errands, their son might not come to see them. Once they were able to state this fear, their son was able to reassure them of his plan to continue his weekly visits.

For Those Who Feel All Alone in the Process of Caring for an Older Family Member and Want Professional Support and Guidance

Margaret has a lot on her plate. She works full-time, has a young child and is an only child of a recently widowed father who has multiple chronic medical conditions. Her primary sense of support is her husband who travels frequently for his work. When everything goes smoothly, her life feels pretty much in balance; however, it doesn't take much to set off the balance, e.g., her daughter getting sick, her father calling her that he has run out of his medicine, her boss telling her of an important deadline, and so on. When her mother was alive, she quite capably attended to Margaret's father's needs. Now that she is gone, the task seems daunting.

The geriatric care manager acts as a support to Margaret. Just knowing that the GCM is there to respond to any problem that may arise provides Margaret with greater peace of mind.

In fact, when her father's neighbor called Margaret recently to let her know that her father had fallen, Margaret called the care manager, who coordinated getting her father to the doctor and reported back the results of the visit. Having the support of the GCM, Margaret did not have to ask her boss for time off or figure out who would pick up her daughter after school.

What Is Geriatric Care Management?

Geriatric care management is an extremely effective service delivery model. It's a process in which a professional (social worker, nurse, psychologist) assesses the situation, develops a plan of care, implements the recommendations, monitors the situation and then reevaluates the situation to ensure that the client's needs are being met while providing support and guidance to all involved in the elder's support system. The process involves five phases.

Phase I: Assessment. During this phase the care manager strives to understand the situation. Through scheduled home visits, the professional care manager meets with the older client and the involved support network to evaluate how a client is managing. The assessment may include personal information and history; health and medication information; insurance, financial and legal information; functional assessment; risk screens for nutrition, memory, depression, abuse, falls, home safety, and caregiver stress.

Phase II: Care plan. During this phase the care manager develops a plan (course of action) with specific recommendations. The care plan typically will identify the concerns/problems/issues and will articulate interventions to meet the agreed-upon objectives of the parent(s) and the family members.

Phase III: Implementation of recommended services. During this phase the action takes place, getting the necessary services in place. Once a care plan is agreed upon, the care manager can work quickly to initiate the recommended services. Services may include home-delivered meals; transportation services; home health services; in-home care; arranging for medical equipment; home adaptations; day care programs; social activities; referrals to legal, financial, medical professionals as needed; and so forth.

Phase IV: Monitoring. During this phase quality is the focus. The care manager tracks the services that are put into place to ensure services are being delivered well and that they are providing the elder with the kind of value as intended to meet the objectives set forth in the care plan.

Phase V: Reevaluation. During this phase measurements and adjustments are made to ensure that the objectives of the plan are met; and as the situation changes, the care plan is adapted to best meet the client's needs at that time.

Who Are the Geriatric Care Managers?

The National Association of Professional Geriatric Care Managers (GCM), based in Tucson, Arizona, is an organization of practitioners whose goal is the advancement of dignified care for the elderly and their families. GCM is committed to maximizing the independence and autonomy of frail elders while striving to ensure that the highest quality and most cost-effective health and human services are used when and where appropriate. Through education, advocacy, counseling, and the delivery of concrete services, GCM members assist older persons and their families in coping with the challenges of aging.

GCM promotes the highest standards of practice. Full membership is open only to qualified individuals with a minimum of a bachelor's degree in the field of human services (social work, psychology, gerontology) or a substantial equivalent (e.g., a registered nurse), who are certified or licensed at the independent practice level and who are experienced in the delivery of services to the elderly and their families.

When selecting a care manager, you may want to consider the following: experience, formal education, training, certification, and professional discipline.

In order to ensure quality services, GCM has developed the following "Pledge of Ethics":

Provision of Service. I will provide ongoing service to you only after I have assessed your needs and you, or a person designated to act for you, understand and agree to a plan of service, the results that may be expected from it, and the cost of service.

Self-Determination. I will base my plan of service on goals you, or a person designated to act for you, have defined, and which enhance the decisions you have made concerning your life.

Loyalty. My first duty is loyalty to you. I will always provide service based on your best interest even if this conflicts with my interests or the interest of others.

Termination of Service. I will end service to you only after reasonable notice. I will recommend a plan for you to continue to receive service as needed.

Substitute Judgment. I will not substitute my judgment for yours unless I am acting in the role of your guardian/conservator, appointed by a court of law, or with your approval or the approval of someone designated to act for you.

Confidentiality. I will hold in trust any confidence you give me, disclosing information to others only with your permission, or if I am compelled to do so by a belief that you will be seriously harmed by my silence, or if the laws of this state require me to do so.

Referrals/Disclosure. I will refer you only to services and organizations I believe to be appropriate and of good quality. I will fully explain to you any business relationship I have with any service I propose, and give you information on alternatives, if at all possible, so that you, or a person designated to act for you, can make an informed decision to accept or reject the services I recommend to you.

Cooperation. I will strive to assure cooperation among all the individuals involved in providing service and care to you.

Qualifications. I am fully qualified in my profession to provide the services I undertake. I continue to improve my skills and knowledge by participating in professional development programs and maintaining certification and licensing in my profession.

Discrimination. I will not promote or sanction any form of discrimination.

CHAPTER 12

The "Dagwood" Generation — Helping Parents Plan

When I was a young social worker, we referred to middle-aged people as part of the "sandwich generation." This generation had to deal with the issue of aging parents while raising their own children.

How times are changing!

Nowadays, we need to talk about a "Dagwood sandwich" (a multidecker sandwich)! It is not uncommon for fifty-year-olds to still be raising teenagers, while also having young grandchildren. At the same time, they may have aging parents who need their help, too. They may feel frustrated and torn.

Utilize the information in this book to help your parents plan sensibly for their long term care needs. Helping them plan properly now can massively reduce the burden on you for years to come.

Encourage your parents to obtain LTCI. Some of my clients have children who offer to pay some or all of the premium. They would rather do this than face a really big cost for care down the line. *This is not only to avoid costs, but to avoid ending up as the caregiver!*

As a gerontologist and social worker, I have some additional tips for you to consider in your dealings with your aging parents:

Let Your Parents Make Their Own Decisions

Let your parents make their own decisions if they are of sound mind. You may even want to encourage them to take more time to consider a big decision, such as a move.

For example:

- *If a parent is recently widowed.* During the first year, many widowed people are so upset that they may make rash decisions, or they may just try to follow the advice of well-meaning friends and family. It is better to encourage them to wait with important decisions until the end of the first year of bereavement.

- *If a parent wants to move out of his or her home to a facility.* First ask him to try it out for a month, at least.

> One client told me that her mother wanted to be in a fancy assisted living facility with her friends. The family said, "Go ahead, just leave the house alone till you try it out." Two weeks later the mother came home. She hated the facility; it was not at all what she had imagined. She was so thankful to be able to return to her own home.

Urge your parents not to sell or empty their house or apartment until they are fully satisfied with the new living arrangement.

> One couple came to consult with me when I was working as a gerontology specialist at a community mental health center, after they had tried to commit suicide. What went wrong?
>
> They had been living in Georgia and their children were in Los Angeles. They decided that they wanted to be near their grandchildren. In Georgia, they lived in a lovely community. They had a beautiful home, were near a golf course, and had many friends and activities. When they left Georgia they sold their home for a low price. They came to L.A. and soon found that their grandchildren had their own lives to lead, and were not often available.

Suddenly they found themselves without their friends and activities. The cost of homes had gone up dramatically in Georgia, and they could not afford to live in that community again. They were lonely and desperate, and realized that they had made a terrible mistake. If only they had kept the home and rented a place in L.A. for a while to try it out… it was too late. There was no going back.

If your loved one decides to make a move, tries it out, and likes it — then support it. If you want her to move and she is not interested — leave her alone.

One client needed to find a new assisted living facility. I got the names of four facilities in her neighborhood. How amazed I was that she didn't care for the one I believed was the nicest — both in looks and in activities. She selected the one I didn't care for at all. Yet I knew that this had to be *her choice*, and if she made the choice herself, she was most apt to make it work for her.

People need to make their own choices.

She May Look a Lot Worse Than She Feels!

When elderly people get sick they often look so bad that the family thinks their life is coming to an end. Pain medication administered after a broken hip or other operation or illness can even (temporarily) cause a person to look terminally ill, or act psychotic.

Don't let crisis management get the better of good sense.

Jean's call was particularly sad. Her mother had been quite ill and it appeared that the end was near. Always efficient, Jean took it upon herself to close her mother's apartment. She took all the little things her mother loved and had saved and threw them out. She put the furniture and TV in her own garage.

To everyone's surprise, Jean's mother got well, and asked to go home. Her apartment was gone. The family could probably find another apartment for her, but none of her personal possessions remained. Jean realized she had made a terrible mistake, and her mother was devastated.

One of my jobs as a social worker is to let people know that a health crisis can be resolved *without* a dramatic change in a person's living situation. Sometimes, a person just needs to be given time to get better.

Whose Problem Is It, Anyway?

This is a question I often asked families when I was doing gerontological social work. Here are some classic cases in which children projected their own discomfort onto their parents:

Example 1. The daughter of an aging woman called me and said, "I want to find a residential care facility for mother."

"What is the problem?" I asked. She replied, "We came to visit Mom and the house looks bad. The paint needs work, and the plumbing is ancient."

"Does it bother your mother?" I asked. "No!" she exclaimed. I told her, "If your mother is happy where she is, at home, let her stay. *The problem is yours, not hers!*"

Example 2. A client called and said he needed a nursing home for his mother. I asked why. He said that his mother was home alone, and he lived in fear that his mother might fall and break her hip.

I explained to him that his mother could fall just as easily in a nursing home (perhaps even more easily in the unfamiliar environment). I also told him that that very day, another woman had called to tell me that *her* mother had fallen in a nursing home and broken her hip! She had slipped on the urine of another patient. The client's worry was *his* problem, not his mother's.

How You Can Help an Elderly Parent

Encourage your parents to be productive and do what they can for others. For example, they may call someone daily to make sure the other person is fine. They should do as much as possible to take care of their own needs as well — they will be better off for it.

Send over a child or grandchild to help your parent do a life review. Make a list of questions the child can ask and have him or her tape and write down the answers. This will give your parent the chance to gain more perspective on a long life. The child will learn a great deal, and this information will be a treasure for the family in the future.

Make sure that your parents have proper food to eat, and/or the supplies to prepare it for themselves. Some elderly people start to live on sweets and prepared foods, and don't eat healthfully. They may not taste food as well as they did when they were younger (hence the increased "sweet tooth"). They need more vitamins than before, and even when they are eating properly they may not absorb the vitamins as well. Great nutrition is the most effective preventative care a person can get.

Utilize the services of a geriatric care manager for a frail parent. A geriatric care manager specializes in assisting older people and their families with long term care arrangements. You may find it helpful to review the care management information, considering how a GCM might benefit your parents.

Try to steer your parent to excellent medical care. Whenever possible, use doctors with geriatric specialization. If your parents are over sixty-five, I recommend that they purchase Medicare along with a Medicare supplement, rather than giving up their Medicare and taking an HMO. When they need a specialist, access to the fullest possible choice of doctors might save their lives.

If you are over sixty-five, you probably know about Medicare supplement policies. If you are under sixty-five, you *should* know about them. No, they won't cover long term care, but they do fill the gaps in Medicare. *Warning:* Some people who have had HMO coverage sign over their Medicare to that HMO, or to another one. *Don't do it.* HMOs, no matter how nice some of the people and doctors are, promise to take care of you for the Medicare allowance alone. It isn't working; HMOs are starting to charge a monthly fee to their members, and you can't always get the specialists you want and need when you are sick. *HMOs limit your choice, which is not in your best interest!*

Old age, by itself, is not a disease! Always look for the underlying cause of a problem. For example, massive strokes can be prevented when doctors look for reasons for sudden falls, which might be caused by "early," minor strokes. Also, many doctors are unaware that older people do poorly on certain medications, and that standard doses may cause complications. Try to find a doctor with some expertise in treating older people.

> Sam was complaining to his doctor about problems with his left knee. The doctor said, "Sam, what do you expect? You're ninety-six years old!" Sam replied, "But my right knee is also ninety-six years old and it doesn't hurt!"

Your parent(s) may be best off in his own home. Some adult children want to be protective and encourage their parent to move in with them. However, parents who prefer their independence may do better in their own home — perhaps with a little bit (or even a lot) of help. There, they will be in charge of their home and their life, and may be much happier.

Facing Reality: Parents Get Older

When we were small, we needed to think of our parents as powerful and immortal. We relied on them for everything — food, shelter, safety, education, emotional and spiritual support. Parents mean everything to a small child, as well they should.

We cannot take that same dream into adulthood, however, refusing to accept the reality that parents get older. We need to let go of the notion — appropriate to a toddler, but not to an adult — that our sanity and survival depend on our parents' health and immortality.

"Death is the tax we pay for loving people." While no one wants to contemplate the loss of a parent, we do need to recognize that life is finite and that death is its inevitable conclusion. It is in the natural order of things that our parents, who gave us life, will pass away.

We need to face that reality head-on instead of denying it, because it doesn't do us or our parents any good to pretend that they are still as young as they were when we first knew them. The most loving thing we can do for our parents is to recognize their vulnerability — and to recognize also that simply by virtue of their age, they are candidates for the sorts of illnesses and accidents we would really rather not think about.

That's why this is the time — now, while making your own plans — to discuss with your parents exactly what sort of care *they* want — exactly how aggressive treatment should be, and where they wish to be treated.

It is vital that your parents also put these instructions in writing, and do so in a legal form that hospitals, caregivers, and other medical practitioners must respect. It frequently happens that different family members have conflicting ideas on how to treat an ailing parent, and even whether treatment should be given at all. How are the doctors and nurses to make a decision if family members themselves cannot agree?

Depending on their age and health, it may be too late for your parents to buy LTCI; it is still important to help them with whatever planning is possible.

In Summary...

1. Parents who are alert and whose minds are clear should be encouraged to make their own decisions.

2. Don't make your problem into theirs. Always ask yourself, "Whose problem is it?"

3. Give older people time to recuperate from an illness before assuming that their life is over, or jumping to conclusions.

4. Use a geriatric care manager to get good ideas for resources and to be available to help your parent when you are not around.

5. Encourage your parents to find good medical care. With their approval, help them find it.

6. If your parents are happy at home, don't urge them to leave... make it possible for them to stay there.

7. Encourage your parents and other aging relatives to put their wishes into writing, and to get LTCI if they can.

STEP THREE:

Putting Your Plans in Writing

CHAPTER 13

An Attorney Helps You Plan

by Caren R. Nielsen, Esq.

This chapter will help you identify legal issues in your family, and will provide you with legal tips on how to make sure that your estate plan and personal health care desires (including the desire to remain at home) will be carried out. This article cannot replace the personal counsel of a legal professional, but it will help guide you through the relevant issues.

One thing to remember is that an individual's level of understanding (referred to as "mental capacity") affects the legal options available to him. People who are young and healthy, older and healthy, or are diagnosed with *early stage* Alzheimer's have the option to plan ahead to avoid the unnecessary crises that often occur without planning.

The best advice I can give you is to put your desires in writing and into legal documents. You may have family members you love or friends you trust, but under the law of many states, the only way to ensure that your individual desires must be followed is to put them in writing. This is because written documents create legally binding instructions and there are consequences when legal instructions are not followed. Also, even if you select a person you trust to carry out your wishes, there is no guarantee that this person will survive you.

The four most important legal documents you can execute to ensure that your personal and financial care desires will be carried out are:

• Advance Health Care Directives

- Powers of Attorney for Finance
- Wills
- Trusts

Advance Health Care Directives

The number one document that you should have is the one that concerns your health care choices and your desires regarding life-support issues. This document may be referred to as a *Living Will*, a *Power of Attorney for Health Care* or an *Advance Health Care Directive*.

A Power of Attorney for Health Care lets you choose in advance who will make your health care decisions if you become unable to make your own decisions. In California, beginning July 1, 2000, a Power of Attorney for Health Care is now called an Advance Health Care Directive. It is a legal document that contains your specific health care wishes, your desires regarding life support, and allows you to nominate another person to speak to doctors on your behalf if you cannot communicate your own medical desires.

An Advance Health Care Directive can also contain *personal care* choices, such as a desire to remain living at home and a desire to spend money on home health care. It also allows you to express your desires concerning organ donation, funeral arrangements and the disposition of your body when you die. In your Advance Health Care Directive, you should name your choice for conservator should you need one.

The Advance Health Care Directive may include specific personal requests such as the following:

- Life support (can be specific: ventilator, intravenous nutrition/hydration; blood transfusions)
- Names of people you want to have visit at the hospital (keep in mind that a family member can otherwise bar a patient's lifelong partner or friend from the hospital room)
- Desire to remain at home
- Desire to donate organs
- Pain medication, even if it means addiction
- To be read to from the Bible, Torah or Koran

- Music, no music, books on tape
- Massages, going outdoors

Although all of the above-listed personal desires can be communicated orally to your family or informally in a letter, only the Advance Health Care Directive is legally binding. In fact, in 1983, two doctors were indicted for manslaughter for accepting oral directions from family members to remove life support when there was no written legal document to uphold the directions!

The bottom line is that instructions expressed by your family about what treatment you want have no legal effect unless written in a legal document. (Frequently, hospitals and physicians will listen to a family member without a written document, but do you want to take that chance?) There are Probate Code statutes and Health and Safety Code statutes which provide that third parties such as hospitals, doctors, nursing homes, and mortuaries must follow the directions in an Advance Health Care Directive. Therefore, by having an Advance Health Care Directive, both you and your family will have peace of mind, and you are more assured that your wishes will be carried out.

> Jennifer is not married and has no children. Her closest friend is her neighbor, Robert. She has two nieces in Idaho, but she does not know them at all. Last year when Jennifer suffered a stroke, the hospital insisted on contacting the nieces to determine Jennifer's medical treatment. The hospital refused to listen to Jennifer's friend Robert because there was no legal document (Advance Health Care Directive) to appoint Robert as Jennifer's agent.

You can buy preprinted Advance Health Care Directive forms, download examples of forms from the Internet, or have attorney-prepared forms. The disadvantage of a preprinted form is that it may not contain all of your personal desires and may not necessarily reflect the most current law. If you meet with an experienced estate planning attorney, he or she will ask you questions and determine which type of form best expresses your own unique personal desires and concerns.

If you do not have an Advance Health Care Directive, hospitals and doctors may have no choice but to utilize every medical device possible to keep you alive, regardless of your quality of life and the terminal condition of your health. For example, a person in the later stages of Alzheimer's disease is often not a good candidate for a feeding tube; without an Advance Directive, a doctor may be required to use one.

> I had a client who was very ill and was repeatedly in and out of the hospital. She had two sons and did not have an Advance Health Care Directive. Her two sons were constantly fighting over the proper treatment for her, and causing many problems for the doctors and hospital staff. You could tell that both sons loved *her*, but disliked *each other*.

> The two fought over whether their mom should live at home or in a facility, who her doctors should be — even whether pills or liquid medicines were better for her!

> One day, the hospital called me and said that one son was insisting on resuscitation, although the doctor was sure that it would break her ribs because she was so frail. The other son did not want the resuscitation. The doctor did not know to whom to listen. It became necessary to get the court system involved simply to direct her care.

Imagine how different her treatment would have been had there been an Advance Health Care Directive! The doctor would have known what type of care she desired. It also would have eliminated the guilt felt by her two sons, and possibly improved their relationship.

Durable Power of Attorney for Finances

A *Power of Attorney* is a legal document in which you (the "principal") appoint another person (an "agent") to handle your finances. It lets you choose someone you know and trust to make your financial decisions if you are ever unable to do so. (The document can also be drafted to be effective during periods when you are out of town, or simply to appoint another person to handle your financial affairs.)

The word *durable* means that the document continues to be effective *even after your incapacity*. A Power of Attorney that takes effect immediately when you sign it is referred to as an *immediate* Power of Attorney. A Power of Attorney that takes effect only when you become incapacitated is called a *springing* Power of Attorney.

If you desire to remain at home as long as possible, then I recommend that you state this desire in both your Advance Health Care Directive and in your Power of Attorney for Finances. The reason is that the choice of where you will live is often based upon financial concerns as well as health concerns.

If you have selected one person to be your health care agent and a different person to be your financial agent, conflicts can arise between money and type of care. What if your health care agent wants you to remain at home, but you do not have long term care insurance and your financial agent refuses to sell assets to keep you at home or refuses to take out a loan? Problems can easily arise that require a court to resolve them.

The advantage of a professionally prepared Power of Attorney for Finances is that it can be personalized to satisfy your needs and desires. For example, your agent is not permitted to make gifts on your behalf unless the Power of Attorney specifically mentions the authority to make gifts. Most preprinted forms do not contain this provision.

Last Will and Testament

A will takes effect only after death. A will directs who gets your property after you die and who will be the executor. Therefore, the executor of your will cannot help you to remain in your home or pay your bills! A professionally written will can ensure that your assets are distributed exactly as you desire. If an estate is worth more than a certain amount ($100,000 in California), then the will must be *proven up* by the court; this is referred to as the *probate* process, a court proceeding that takes from six months to several years to complete.

In California, there are only three types of valid wills: *statutory, holographic* and *formal.*

A *formal will* requires two witnesses to its execution. In California, a will should never be notarized. To avoid potential conflicts, the witnesses should not be people who are mentioned in the will.

A *statutory will* is a specific form will approved by the legislature in which you fill in the blanks. Although this form will is simple, it is not recommended because you cannot modify the form whatsoever. Most people will desire some modifications and thereby risk invalidating the entire will!

> One client had lived with his girlfriend for more than forty years. He used the statutory will form and on the line for "spouse" he crossed out the word "spouse" and wrote his girlfriend's name. Since the form was modified, the judge wanted to throw out the will, thereby leaving the entire estate to the client's children. The girlfriend succeeded in fighting the judge's initial interpretation, but it cost her $35,000 to do so!

In California, if the value of the estate is under $100,000, no probate will be necessary. (There is an affidavit procedure by which assets can be transferred.)

Helpful hint: A will can also serve to avoid the need for a guardian of the estate if you have minor children.

One thing that many people do not know is that certain assets are not covered by a will, even if you want them to be. These assets include life insurance, joint tenancy, IRAs, pensions, and trust assets.

In summary, keep in mind the following about wills:

1. Wills are less expensive, involve less paperwork, and are less complicated than living trusts
2. You get to choose who inherits your property, including your one-half of community property
3. A will prevents arguments and alleviates burdens among surviving heirs
4. You can establish a trust for minors, spouse, disabled beneficiaries, or others in a will
5. A will gives you the ability to accomplish estate tax planning
6. A will gives you the ability to nominate an executor (remember, a will takes effect only after death)
7. A will enables one to nominate guardians for minor children
8. A will can permit custodian accounts for minors and avoid the need for guardianship of the estate
9. Remember: a will does not avoid probate

10. Requirements: formal wills require two witnesses (not a notary); holographic wills require no witnesses and the signature and "material provisions" must be in the testator's handwriting

Trusts

A *trust* is a written agreement between an owner of assets and a person who will manage the assets held in the trust (trustee). *You can be both parties.* (See Appendix C for more information on Care Management Trusts.)

A trust combines the function of a will and a Power of Attorney for Finances. Like a will, a trust directs who inherits your property after your death. However, unlike a will, a trust also provides for the management of your assets during your life if you should become incapacitated.

You do not lose control of your assets by creating a trust! In fact, you have more control because your wishes are written down for others to follow in case of an emergency. In the trust document, you retain the rights to revoke, to change beneficiaries, to amend, and to terminate the trust. You can change the terms at your discretion at any time you choose. You decide who the trustees (managers) will be, and how your assets are managed.

In a trust document, you can also provide for your beneficiaries in whatever manner you feel to be best, such as periodic payments to beneficiaries at specific ages, ongoing gifts, lifetime support, and so forth.

A trust will generally cost more than a will to prepare and involves more paperwork. *The advantages of having a trust include the following:*

1. To avoid conservatorship (in the event of incompetence)
2. To avoid probate (at death)
3. To postpone death tax until death of surviving spouse
4. To save death taxes at the death of the surviving spouse (Do not use a simple will. Use an A-B or A-B-C trust plan. Contact an attorney for guidance.)
5. To avoid or minimize a second tax called the generation skipping transfer (GST) tax
6. To prevent a surviving spouse from disinheriting the deceased spouse's side of the family

7. To preserve control over estate (e.g.: in a family business; until beneficiaries are mature enough to manage estate; in case of incapacity; control property after death)
8. To maintain privacy. Generally a trust is not subject to probate or other court proceedings. Thus, your personal matters are kept private, known only to those people named in the trust.

The law now requires that all beneficiaries receive notice and a copy of the trust (if requested) once a trust becomes irrevocable, e.g., at death.

Helpful hint: Unlike a simple will, a trust provides estate tax advantages. If you are married and have more than $1.3 million, a very simple A-B trust can save your heirs $190,000 that would otherwise go to the IRS if you did not have a trust.

Joint Tenancy

An asset *held in joint tenancy*, whether real estate, bank accounts, or personal property, becomes the property of the surviving joint tenant automatically on the death of the other joint tenant. Although this is a simple way to transfer property, it is not the best way.

Joint tenancy title does avoid probate. However, you can lose control of your property and sometimes even lose the property itself through joint tenancy title.

Helpful hint: Do not put your children's names on the deed to your house or on bank accounts as a way of estate planning!

Helpful hint: One joint tenant can change the joint tenancy character of property without giving notice to the other joint tenants; thus, there is no guarantee that your goals regarding who will inherit the property will be carried out.

Gift Giving

You may want to give major gifts to your loved ones during your lifetime. These gifts may include your house, stocks, bonds, and/or large sums of money. There are advantages to making gifts, such as the joy of the donor and recipient, a decrease in the value of the donor's estate, and a decrease in estate taxes. However, there are also unintended disadvantages of making gifts, such as:

- Your gift may be attached (taken) by creditors of the recipient.
- Your gift may generate federal gift taxes.
- Your gift may increase capital gains taxes for the donee.
- The gift may disqualify the donor from Medicaid benefits.
- An unintended in-law may inherit your property.

Helpful hint: You may make gifts of up to $10,000 annually to as many people as you wish and a one-time gift of up to $675,000 (during life or at death) without having to pay gift tax.

Helpful hint: Always obtain legal advice before giving away your assets or making any major gifts.

Conservatorships

A *conservatorship* is a court proceeding that appoints another person to make the financial decisions and/or health care decisions for someone who is no longer able to make the decisions him- or herself.

If you become unable to take care of yourself, a conservator may be appointed by the court to take care of you (your person) and/or your money and possessions (your estate). Your conservator may be a relative, close friend, or a professional conservator.

The consequences of a conservatorship are: the court becomes a "part of your family" and monitors all spending decisions and personal care decisions; the conservator chooses where you reside; limitations may be imposed on your independent actions.

A conservator makes many decisions for you, including where you live, what medical care you will receive and how your money is managed.

For many families, a conservatorship can be extremely helpful because it provides protection against financial and physical abuse by requiring court-monitored accountings and supervision.

For other families, however, a conservatorship is a large expense and an intrusion into their private lives. *Proper planning can usually eliminate the need for a conservator. By signing a few documents, you can maintain control of your life even if you become too sick or disabled to make important decisions for yourself.*

Conservatorships can generally be avoided when you have a trust, a health power of attorney and a financial power of attorney.

Get Professional Advice

Let me tell you what most people do: They do nothing until they are faced with a crisis. The problem with the "do nothing" approach is that when a crisis occurs, there are fewer options available and you may not be in a position to communicate your personal wishes to others.

Estate and personal planning can be confusing, even overwhelming. Do not rely on the advice of well-meaning friends and relatives to properly plan for your care and estate. Be sure to consult with an experienced professional in the estate planning, long term care field or elder law field.

Remember, one of the greatest advantages to having an Advance Health Care Directive, Powers of Attorney and a will or trust is that the documents create a network of people, of your choice, who can carry out your plans for you.

Two basic rules to ensure that your desires will be followed are:

1. Put your desires in writing.
2. It is never too soon to prepare your Powers of Attorney, your will and your trust.

The more thought and planning you give to this topic, the greater peace of mind you and your loved ones will have.

CHAPTER 14

Long Term Care Due Diligence for Professional Financial Advisers

by Stephen A. Moses

Never have so many professionals given such bad advice to such damaging effect to so many people than today's financial advisers on long term care planning. Only a rare few lawyers, accountants, and financial planners understand this critical subject in all its ramifications. Fewer still advise the public wisely and objectively, disregarding personal financial advantage. To date, most advisers have not been held to legal or professional account for giving bad advice about long term care. This safe harbor of public ignorance and judicial indifference will not continue much longer, however.

More than ever before — and even more so in the future — financial professionals must understand the risks and costs of long term care and the consequences of poor counsel and inadequate planning. Here's a primer.

Long term care for chronic illness or frailty is the single biggest financial risk most older Americans face. Studies indicate that 43 percent of people over the age of sixty-five will spend some time in a nursing home and that 9 percent will spend five years or more. At an average annual cost of $55,000 per year today and much more in the future, a long term nursing home stay can quickly devastate a family financially. Even the popular new option of "assisted living" averages $25,000 per year. Most seniors' preferred alternative — to receive care in their own homes — can easily exceed the cost of institutional care when a patient requires more than a few hours of assistance per day. The supply of free care from spouses and adult children is dwindling as more and more women — the traditional caregivers — enter the workplace. Thus, a growing number of older Americans will become increasingly dependent on professional long term care services just as the cost of these services skyrockets.

But this is nothing new so far. Almost everyone knows, at least intellectually, that long term care is a big, expensive risk. What most people do not realize is that America's long term care service delivery and financing system is a disastrous mess. Seven major nursing facility chains have declared Chapter 11 bankruptcy. Between 10 and 20 percent of all nursing home beds in the country are in bankrupt facilities today. Hundreds of home health agencies have gone under financially. Many new assisted living facilities are filling far more slowly than anticipated. Long term care stock prices are down precipitously. New capitalization by debt or equity is almost nonexistent for publicly held long term care companies. Caregivers are in desperately short supply, whether they are low-wage nurses' aides in long term care facilities, or unpaid friends and family in private homes. Formal long term care services are too expensive for most Americans to afford, but Medicare and Medicaid pay too little to assure quality home or nursing home care. Litigation against nursing homes and assisted living facilities for providing allegedly poor care is on the rise and is driving liability insurance premiums through the roof.

Only 7 percent of seniors, and virtually none of the baby boomers, own private insurance, which could help them pay the catastrophic cost of long term care. America's gigantic and rapidly aging baby-boom generation guarantees that the challenge of long term care will become greater and far more expensive with time. As of now, long term care is well on its way to trumping Social Security and Medicare as our country's most challenging social problem.

A Country in Denial

Given this reality, one would think most Americans should be aggressively seeking professional advisers and financial products to protect themselves from the huge and growing risks of long term care. But that is just not happening. *The country is in denial.* "Won't happen to me; never go to one of those places; shoot myself first" is the common refrain. Yet — given the fact that half of all people over the age of eighty-five already have Alzheimer's disease — when the time comes, most ailing seniors won't remember why they bought the gun!

What is going on? How is it that the risk and cost of long term care is so high, while the public's concern about this risk is so low?

A System in Crisis

The answer is simple, but rarely understood. For the past thirty-five years, Americans have been able to ignore the risk of long term care, avoid the premiums for private insurance, and wait to see if they ever need expensive professional long term care. When they do require care, they can and do routinely transfer most of the cost to Medicaid, Medicare, and to the financially strapped long term care providers who rely on those fiscally starved government programs for most of their revenue. Precisely why and how this happens is a subject for another article. For now, all that matters is that most people who fail to plan for long term care end up in nursing homes on Medicaid (public welfare). That is what has anesthetized the public to the financial risk of long term care.

Today, however, our welfare-financed, institution-based long term care system is failing and the public has not yet realized that this safety net of the past will no longer be adequate in the future. They have not awakened to the reality that preferred alternatives for long term care like quality home care and assisted living require the ability to pay privately. To be able to pay privately without potentially catastrophic expense requires the foresight to plan early, save, invest, or insure for long term care costs. *The only alternatives are to risk severe financial exposure or rely on publicly financed nursing home care if chronic long term illness strikes.*

Today, we are in a transitional phase between the collapse of America's traditional long term care system and the public's awakening to this danger. Unfortunately, the professional financial advisers who should be alerting the public to these new risks have largely reneged on that responsibility.

Professional Obligations

Under the current circumstances, we should expect every responsible professional financial adviser — including attorneys, CPAs, and financial planners — to urge anyone and everyone who will listen to prepare to pay privately for long term care in the future. Some give such advice, but alas, most don't. Many financial advisers are simply no more aware of the risks of long term care than the people they advise, and for the same reasons. Someone must pay for long term care, they assume, because we don't see thousands of Alzheimer's patients wandering unattended in America's streets.

Who pays? Who knows? Medicaid, Medicare or Santa Claus? Who cares? That is the attitude and it is understandable. The vast majority of all professional long term care services are indeed paid for by Medicaid or Medicare and the proportion of long term care costs borne "out-of-pocket" by private citizens has gone steadily down over the years, as government financing has steadily increased. We might be able to excuse as reasonable the ignorance of advisers who fail to comprehend the need for long term care planning if it were not that the consequences are becoming so grave.

Neither Understandable nor Forgivable

The behavior of many other financial counselors is neither understandable nor forgivable. These are the "Medicaid estate planners" who advise clients not to save, invest, insure, or pay privately for long term care, but rather to impoverish themselves artificially for the purpose of qualifying for Medicaid nursing home benefits.

This practice is doubly damaging. It injures the client *and* the long term care system. Medicaid is a means-tested public assistance program. It is welfare, intended as a safety net for the genuinely needy. The program has a dismal reputation for problems of access, quality, reimbursement, discrimination, and institutional bias.

Someone who retains personal wealth can purchase red-carpet access to top-quality care in the private marketplace at the most appropriate level — home care, assisted living, or nursing home care. Once that wealth has been shifted to heirs by a complicit attorney or financial planner, however, the client becomes dependent on nursing home care financed by a welfare program that pays so little (often less than the cost of care) that it is bankrupting America's service delivery industry.

Is it possible that credentialed financial professionals are giving advice of this kind to the public in America today? *Yes.* In fact, this may be the most common advice provided by attorneys, accountants, financial planners, and many insurance agents (who market annuities as a Medicaid planning device) throughout the United States.

One survey found that "…a majority of [financial planners] felt that an individual with a catastrophic illness should consider transferring assets to family members in order to qualify for Medicaid."

An attorney advises: …if the individual happens to have about $82 million lying around, he or she could even buy a painting by Renoir to hang on the walls of the house… [which he called] burying money in the treasure chest of the house. (A home and all contiguous property regardless of value is exempt for purposes of determining Medicaid nursing home eligibility, as is a business including the capital and cash flow of unlimited value.)

A best-selling self-help book on Medicaid planning suggests: "So is there any practical way to juggle assets to qualify for Medicaid — before losing everything? The answer is yes! By following the tips on these pages, an older person or couple can save most or all of their savings, despite our lawmakers' best efforts… Here are the best options: Hide money in exempt assets… Transfer assets directly to children tax-free… Pay children for their help… Juggle assets between spouses… Pass assets to children through a spouse… Transfer a home while retaining a life estate… Change wills and title to property… Write a Durable Power of Attorney… Set up a Medicaid trust… Get a divorce.…"

Unbelievable? Web sites and public seminars providing similar advice abound. *It seems the big bucks in long term care are to be made by promoting a free ride on public assistance* (usually with the help of expensive professional advice) rather than by convincing people to take responsibility for their own long term care and shoulder the burden of years of personal saving or insurance premiums.

Whether professional advisers are merely ignorant of long term care risks or actively culpable by providing irresponsible, self-serving advice to clients, the consequences for the public are the same.

People who fail to save, invest, or insure for long term care end up dependent on Medicaid nursing home care whether they spend down into impoverishment or dodge the spend-down liability with the help of a Medicaid planner.

What They Don't Tell You...

The gerontological literature on the access and quality deficiencies of Medicaid-financed nursing home care is extensive. People dependent on Medicaid often have a harder time finding a nursing home bed and confront longer waiting lists than private payers. Quality of care in nursing homes heavily dependent on Medicaid financing is often questionable. Medicaid rarely pays for home care or assisted living, which most seniors prefer, and when it does pay, it pays so little that access and quality are suspect. Because nursing homes need full-pay private patients to balance the low-pay Medicaid majority, they often discriminate — legally or otherwise — by providing better rooms, food, or amenities to private payers than to Medicaid residents.

Finally, after the patient dies, every state Medicaid program in the country is required by federal law to seek recovery of all benefits paid from any remaining estate, including a home that was exempt while the patient was alive. Someday heirs and loved ones of ill-advised elders are going to turn with a vengeance on professional advisers who failed to give good advice or actively promulgated bad planning options. That day is coming sooner rather than later.

We already see the tip of the iceberg of potential malpractice risk regarding long term care due diligence. Twelve years ago, one expert wrote:

> During the last thirty years, the number of suits alleging attorney malpractice in an estate planning context has skyrocketed.... The malpractice revolution has begun. The defenses of privacy and the statute of limitations have been routed. Different types of errors in estate planning are coming under judicial scrutiny. Many other errors are ripe for such scrutiny.

More recently and specifically, another writer warned:

> Many of the appellate decisions in the attorney malpractice field involve cases brought by the former clients — and nonclients — of elder law attorneys... The most frequently litigated legal issue in cases against elder law attorneys concerns the question: To whom did the attorney owe a duty [i.e., the vulnerable senior or the heir with a conflict of interest]?...

A related question is whether an attorney has an obligation to inform his or her client of subsequent events that have an impact on the estate plan (e.g., amendments to Medicaid laws and regulations or changes in family circumstances that render moot or ineffective provisions in testamentary instruments).

In 1999, an article in the *Elder Law Journal* admonished:

> Attorneys who represent elderly clients, or who wish to expand into this rapidly growing area of the law, have a professional responsibility to advise their clients of the available funding options and of the consequences of not planning for the contingency of prolonged and expensive LTC.... Attorneys who advise clients about future financial security and concerns fulfill their professional obligation when they provide informed counsel in the area of LTC....

> If [attorneys] are not informed about the nuances of LTC insurance, they may be held liable if a client sues them for negligence. In our litigation-prone society, there are few professions or occupations outside of medicine and public accounting where the practitioner is so exposed to risk. Hence, it is in their own self-interest that lawyers consider all options when planning for medical, financial, and quality of life decisions for elderly clients.

Although the foregoing quotations address the malpractice vulnerability of lawyers specifically, the principles apply equally to any and all professional financial advisers. Certainly, accountants and CPAs have a similar fiduciary responsibility to their clients with regard to long term care risk and expense. Even insurance agents with no other professional designation would be well advised to keep their errors and omissions coverage paid up, especially if they recommend annuities for the purpose of Medicaid planning.

In summary, many professional financial advisers in the United States have given, are giving, and will probably continue to give very bad advice about long term care planning. Many ignore altogether the emotional and financial consequences of failing to plan for long term care. At least, perhaps, these careless advisers know not what they do. Others, however, address the issue of asset protection in a manner that leaves infirm seniors impoverished and vulnerable to inferior, publicly financed nursing home care. These advisers use their professional acumen to grant an early inheritance to their clients' heirs while pulling down a big fee for themselves.

Both kinds of advisers — the ignorant and the irresponsible — bear a professional responsibility to learn the facts and mend their ways. The consequences for clients of both are the same — welfare dependency, loss of independence, and health care vulnerability. When the prestigious *New York Times* editorializes on this issue, as quoted below, malpractice suits and stern judicial scrutiny cannot be far behind. It upbraids

> the blatant and often unethical misuse of the [Medicaid] program by well-to-do patients in nursing homes. These patients exploit legal loopholes to transfer their wealth to their children, thus technically impoverishing themselves and providing themselves with inexpensive nursing home care. What was supposed to be a program for the poor has turned into a boondoggle for everyone else…. The system is a scandal. (April 14, 1996)

Due professional diligence in the field of long term care requires that all professional advisers (1) understand the consequences of failure to save, invest, or insure for long term care; (2) advise their clients candidly of these dangers; and (3) recommend responsible financial tools to prevent such negative outcomes. In many or even most instances, the best alternative for advisers who are generalists may be to recognize that long term care is a highly specialized field and refer clients to trusted experts in that specialty.

All of the arguments and facts in this article are thoroughly documented and substantiated in reports and articles published by the Center for Long Term Care Financing. This article was commissioned by The Constellation Group, a financial planning firm in West Hartford, Connecticut, /www.theconstellationgroup.com/. Reprinted with permission.

STEP FOUR:
Finding an Ally

CHAPTER 15

No One Can Do It Alone

Let's talk for a moment about courage.

What if doctors and hospital staff all insist that you are in need of nursing home placement? If you are unable to defend yourself in a crisis, will your daughter or son be able to withstand the pressure? Or will they fold under "doctor knows best," even when "doctor" advises placement in a facility? Even with all your planning, you could still be at risk for institutionalization.

Psychological studies show that it is difficult to stand up to many others unless one has an ally. This is true even when a person has complete conviction that he is correct. Without at least one ally, most people will succumb to the pressure to conform to expectations.

You need to take just one more small step.

> When my father had a stroke and all the hospital staff opposed my plans to take him home, I had the advantage of knowing *absolutely*, based on my years of research, that the very best care my father could get would be one-on-one care at home. I was very fortunate to have a husband who totally supported me. Believe me, it was not easy to disagree with the whole hospital staff (who repeatedly insisted that they, in their wisdom, knew better than I).

If I, a trained social worker and gerontologist, found it difficult, you can assume that your family will, too. *I urge you to find a doctor who will agree to support your wishes.*

Having an ally in a white coat can give your family the courage to succeed in carrying out the plans you have so carefully put in place.

In addition to your doctor (who might be your general practitioner, or a specialist such as a cardiologist, pulmonologist, endocrinologist, or the like), you'll also want to include as allies your lawyer and your accountant. Get as many of your professionals as possible into your corner.

If my gift to you is guidance in long term care planning, the decorative ribbons are your allies. They will make things oh-so-much nicer, and help to hold the gift together by giving your family (or care manager) the extra courage they may need to completely fulfill your wishes.

Getting Organized

CHAPTER 16

Reviewing the Four-Step Solution

Given the right advance planning, financial resources, and encouragement, living life at home is possible for most people who might otherwise end their lives in nursing homes.

Of course, this requires careful planning. To alleviate family strain, make a plan that includes hiring others to do all the direct care. The family can supervise, help with arrangements and shopping, and enjoy visiting. The earlier your plans are put into place, the greater the chance that your wishes can and will be honored.

What Do I Do Now?

To plan ahead to stay home, consider the following:

Step 1: Long Term Care Insurance

- Set up a financial arrangement clearly specifying that the funds are intended for the sole purpose of home care. This arrangement should include long term care insurance and your own assets. (A good LTCI broker and attorney will help you with this.)

Step 2: Geriatric Care Management

- Try to appoint at least one family member locally who is capable of hiring and supervising caregivers. Otherwise, hire a geriatric care manager, friend, relative, or other person who can organize this. (Your long term care insurance may cover some of the cost of the care manager, and some insurance companies have care managers on staff or use third-party care managers to assist in these matters.) You can hire a geriatric care manager of your own in advance on a retainer, to be available in an emergency. Speak with the person ahead of time and communicate your wishes.

- Select another person to shop for food, medical supplies and drugs, order equipment, make doctors' appointments, and make other care decisions. This can be a family member, friend, or hired person.

Step 3: Put Your Wishes into Writing

- Select an attorney who specializes in estate planning to help you with your plan.
- Prepare documents now so that your wishes will be carried out. State your desire to stay at home no matter what happens, and explain how this will be funded. Give the power of attorney to someone you trust to follow your wishes without being swayed by other financial considerations. Sometimes even close family members who have been chosen to handle these types of affairs on behalf of an incapacitated relative want to save money and effort and choose an institution over a home setting. This conflict of interest can be avoided if the cost of care is covered by long term care insurance.
- Have a living will. Consult your religious leader for guidance as to the recommendations of your particular faith. If you are Jewish, have a *halachic* will — a will made in keeping with Jewish law — stating which rabbi to call when there are difficult decisions to make about feeding, resuscitation, and other life-and-death issues. (Information on obtaining forms for a *halachic* will is found at the end of this book.)

Step 4: Find an Ally

- Be sure your family doctor fully supports your wishes, will back you up, and will send you home to recuperate after hospitalization.

Getting Organized

In caring for my own father, I found it a strain to keep track of the myriad details regarding resources, doctors, prescriptions, phone numbers and other data. My assistant and I devised a portable file system tailored to manage this type and quantity of information. We used an accordion-type folder, divided into many sections (these folders are easily found in office supply stores, or even large drugstores). The folder includes sections for prescriptions, resources, living will, doctors (names, addresses, and phone numbers), medical cards, and the many other bits of data we needed to locate promptly.

You can set up your own system in advance, in the event that you or a loved one suddenly becomes incapacitated. In fact, when you realize how practical this system is for coordinating your day-to-day health needs, you may want to start using it at once! A system which consolidates all pertinent information into a manageable package makes coordination of health and care needs much less stressful.

Start a system now to organize these materials and others, so that if there is a sudden medical crisis you will be prepared. Be sure to include a section with your LTCI contract, legal documents, information on whom to call in an emergency, and phone numbers of your doctors, family members, and the geriatric care manager (if you have preselected someone). This file can be picked up in a hurry by you, your spouse, or your loved ones as they rush to the hospital to be with you.

You and your family will have all the required information right at hand the minute it's needed.

Letter Prototype

This is a prototype of a letter to put at the front of the portable file you will make available to your family.

To my family (or geriatric care manager),

This file has been set up to give you guidance in the event of a health crisis, if I am unable to express my wishes, or am too weak to carry them out.

In the legal section you will find my wishes in writing. Also included are the legal papers including the advance health care directive, living will… (include all pertinent documents).

In the Long Term Care Insurance section is a copy of my contract, and information on how to reach the company if I need to make a claim.

The Geriatric Care Management section includes information on how to find a geriatric care manager or includes the name of one I have already chosen. I wish to have this person contacted as soon as possible, so that he or she can set in action my plans to have care given to me at home.

Other sections include:

Important phone numbers, including my attorney, accountant and/or financial manager, doctors, geriatric care manager, pharmacy, family members, long term care insurance broker, phone number of my long term care insurance company claims department, friends who can be of help, and so on.

A list of my medications.

Medicare card and Medigap (Medicare supplement) policy card, or other health insurance card.

Please make a list of people who are helpful to me and put it in this file, so we can thank them after the crisis is over.

Love, Mom and Dad

Better Five Years Too Soon Than Five Minutes Too Late

It makes enormous sense to create a care plan well in advance. Many people say, "Better five years too soon than five minutes too late," and I agree wholeheartedly.

It's a four-step plan, but the peace of mind that you will enjoy as a result is *incalculable*. You'll rest assured knowing that if something serious happens, you are prepared.

It's that simple.

CHAPTER 17

The Gift to You, Your Spouse, and Your Family

We've reached the end of our journey together. I've frequently made reference to long term care planning as a gift because I believe strongly that it is a gift. It is a gift for your spouse, because it relieves him or her of the financial, emotional, and physical burdens that come with being the primary caregiver if something should happen to you. It's a gift to yourself, because you can enjoy peace of mind for years, knowing that if serious health issues strike, you'll be able to live in dignity on your own terms. You'll be spared the agony of spending, in a few short years, the financial resources you worked so hard to attain.

Consider, too, what a gift you'll be giving to your children. They may not even want to think about their parents getting old, so when you first broach the subject of long term care they may not want to talk about it. *When they understand how you've protected yourself and your spouse, they will be gratified beyond measure.*

Invite your family to visit you. Sit down around the table. Tell them about the planning you have done. Take out the portable file you've created that contains your important papers, and show them its contents.

Tell them that you have discussed this with your doctor and lawyer, who are willing to support you and help you to stay home rather than go to a nursing home.

Explain what a favor you are doing for them. When a crisis occurs, your children will not have to read your mind to figure out what you want... or worse, disagree among themselves. They will not have to give up their chances for advancement at work due to caregiving responsibilities. If they are older, they will not be put under terrible physical and emotional stress by having to provide care for you themselves. They will not have to live in fear that you will use up all of your assets and end up having to go to a nursing home because there is nothing left but Medicaid to rely upon. They may even receive an inheritance, someday!

Everyone Wins

Your children will be able to count on a geriatric care manager to help set up and manage your care; they will feel proud that you are at home and comfortable; and they will be able to relax and travel, enjoy their own children, and enjoy other interests, without having to stay constantly by your side.

And if your children say, "Don't worry, we'll care for you and pay for it" — don't listen to them. *They have no idea how much it costs — financially, physically, emotionally — to provide long term care.* You do. You may even wish to give your family a copy of this book to help them understand what you have given them. Some well-meaning children do try to give care, and either give up entirely and institutionalize a parent, or continue to give the care themselves and destroy their own lives. That's not the legacy you wish to leave to the ones you love most.

Some people may say, "You may die suddenly and never need care!" Or, "You're better off saving for old age yourself." They will assure you that nursing homes are fine, "You'll be so sick you won't even care." If you have your eyes open, then you know better. It is true that there are no guarantees, and this plan is not for everyone. But if you follow this advice, you will very likely succeed, and you will find that your long term future will afford you the dignity you want for yourself.

Everyone wins.

⌣

Ultimately, we are all in this together. My purpose in writing this book is to help you, and help others, as well. So please, let me know what you find most helpful, and share with me new things you learn as you go along. I would truly love to hear your story and consider sharing any advice you might offer… perhaps in a future book on long term care. I look forward to hearing from you.

Religion and Euthanasia

I don't claim to have ESP, but so often when I am working with clients on the subject of long term care insurance, I feel as though I can read their minds.

They're looking at the list of things that can go terribly wrong with the human body — strokes, Alzheimer's, dementia — and they're thinking, "This could never happen to me. But if it does, I'll shoot myself rather than lie there like a vegetable."

Frequently they actually say as much to me. That horror of physical or mental incapacitation is so universal as to deserve a serious response in this book.

We've been concentrating on the practical side of things so far, and now it's time to turn to the spiritual aspects in coping with a life-threatening crisis. There are ethical implications of how we treat our parents and ourselves as we reach the end of our lives.

The purpose of this chapter is to help those who have not yet made a decision to sort out their feelings about this complex, emotion-laden issue. It's called an "Afterword," yet it's a very important part of this book.

⤙

The first thing to realize is that when people *do* become seriously incapacitated, they usually aren't thinking about ending their misery by killing themselves. They're thinking about what they can do to get better.

Most people don't want to die.

New studies, published in the *Journal of the American Medical Association*, show that while 60 percent of terminally ill cancer patients surveyed said that euthanasia should be a legal option — only 10 percent of them even considered it for *themselves* when they learned of their diagnosis. Two to six months later, half of those who did consider ending their own lives because of their illness had abandoned the idea.[9]

When individuals lose the physical or mental capacity to perform the activities of daily living referred to in long term insurance policies — transferring, eating, bathing, toileting, and the like — that whole notion of "I'll do myself in" usually vanishes. Although, while we are healthy, we might think that we'd rather die than live without dignity, when illness strikes, the vast majority of people suddenly find an enormous amount of dignity in remaining alive — and recovering as quickly and completely as possible.

Studies have shown again and again that the desire to end life is almost always a result of depression, and can generally be attributed to a lack of community. People with family and friends who value them don't usually want to kill themselves.

⌒

> Claire said, "I told my husband that if I ever get that sick, to
> just put me out of my misery, and he got so upset with me.
> Why?"

There are at least three reasons why a spouse would be upset by that kind of statement.

The *first* is that no one wants to even contemplate the death of one's spouse or loved one, let alone think about causing it. The *second* is that when we love people, we continue to value them, even when they need our help. The *third* answer is somewhat more surprising, and it is the focus of the remainder of this chapter.

Even people who do not describe themselves as religious feel bothered on some level by the prospect of themselves or a loved one "doing themselves in" in the event of serious infirmity. What is the cause of that discomfort?

I don't usually answer that question in the setting of the insurance office, but I'd like to discuss it with you now.

Many of the world's great religions affirm the doctrine that it is not within the rights of humans to take a life — one's own or someone else's. Religions teach that human beings are created in the image of God, but that message has become obscured today. We live in a media culture where someone can actually get away with killing a human being on live television. The power of religion has been diminished considerably by the power of the media, which seeks thrills (and ratings) with little or no regard for morality.

Within us there remains that still, small voice telling us that there really is some sort of moral basis for the decision to preserve life.

- The *traditional Christian belief* concerning all forms of suicide was summed up by Thomas Aquinas in the thirteenth century. Suicide, he wrote, violates one's natural desire to live and harms other people. Since life is the gift of God, it is only to be taken by God.

- The *Greek Orthodox* Archdiocese of America made its opposition clear in a 1996 statement to any form of "suicide, euthanasia…, regardless if it is cloaked in terms like 'death with dignity.'"

- The catechism of the *Roman Catholic Church* similarly states that "we are obliged to accept life gratefully and preserve it for His honor… We are stewards, not owners, of the life God has entrusted to us. It is not ours to dispose of."

Pope John Paul II, in his 1995 encyclical letter *"Against the Culture of Death,"* reaffirms this point. The pontiff writes:

> [T]here exists in contemporary culture a certain Promethean attitude which leads people to think that they can control life and death by taking the decisions about them into their own hands. What really happens in this case is that the individual is overcome and crushed by a death deprived of any meaning or hope.

We see a tragic expression of all this in the spread of euthanasia — disguised and surreptitious, or practiced openly and even legally. As well as for reasons of a misguided pity at the sight of the patient's suffering, euthanasia is sometimes justified by the utilitarian motive of avoiding costs which bring no return and which weigh heavily on society.

- The Union of *Orthodox Jewish* Congregations of America filed a comment with the United States Supreme Court in 1997 supporting laws banning physician-assisted suicide:

  This is an issue of critical constitutional and moral significance which Jewish tradition clearly speaks to. We believe that the recognition of a constitutionally recognized right to die for the terminally ill is a clear statement against the recognition and sanctity of human life.

Rabbi David Lapin, rabbi emeritus of the Pacific Jewish Center in Venice, California, notes that the starting point for the question of euthanasia is the fact that man is created in God's image. Rabbi Lapin writes:

God created man in His own image. God has no *physical* image, yet there is something in the appearance and aura of a human that contains godliness. When one is in the presence of a great human being, one tangibly experiences that godliness.

"You will not murder" is the sixth of the Ten Commandments. When you look at the two tablets of the Ten Commandments, you see side by side "I am the Lord your God" (the first commandment) and "You will not murder" (the sixth). This is because in murdering a man, you deprive the world of that man's godliness.

Our bodies are not our property to do with as we wish: Our bodies are entrusted to us for use in the service of God and the good of humankind. Our bodies are more than us. They express a dimension of divinity over which we have no ownership. For this reason even after our lives are over, our bodies retain a certain sanctity with which we may not interfere. (That is why Jews may not will themselves to be cremated.)

Terminating life is murder even if it is done with the victim's permission. Thus the term "euthanasia" is a euphemism for *murder*. [Murder can sometimes even be committed by an act of omission: for example, not providing for the reasonable needs (not heroic measures) of a sick or injured person is murder if that omission leaves him or her dead, irrespective of how close to death the person was.]

If we take God out of the equation, where do we stop? Is it an individual decision that a man decides to take control over ending his own life? Or is it a family decision? Or a societal decision? In a dictatorship, the dictator decides who will live and who will die. In a democracy, the majority might vote that all persons terminally ill should be killed, as a matter of expediency and efficiency. Or perhaps all people over age seventy should be killed, to preserve societal resources. How about killing all persons of a particular religion, color or race? Perhaps only the strongest should be allowed to live.

Right and wrong exist only granted that there is a God Who has instilled in every human being a sacred, divine soul.

This issue hangs not only between you and the victim, it is between you and the entire world. Who knows what impact that person might have had either consciously or unconsciously, even in the very last moments of life? In a powerful moment at the end of a dying person's life, he or she may see the truth with a clarity that can send a flicker of prayer through his or her mind that can change the world.

We have no right to deprive the world of the possibility of that transformation.

Rabbi Lapin's statement on euthanasia offers a perspective that is often ignored in our society: a spiritual perspective. It explains why so many people feel a discomfort they cannot name when it comes to this whole business of "doing themselves in" should they become incapacitated.

For those who share the view that passive euthanasia is morally wrong, long term care insurance presents an even more attractive possibility, since LTCI makes it possible for a person to be cared for in dignity and at home, at almost any level of health. Long term care insurance is a method of *preserving* life, in keeping with the Ten Commandments and with the dictates of religion. LTCI provides the financial and emotional resources to preserve in a dignified manner lives that might otherwise be terminated prematurely.

Obviously, this topic is not a simple one. It is a complex and deeply emotional issue for many. The thoughts expressed here represent an important aspect of the need to take care of ourselves and those we love. I hope this chapter has assisted you in the process of considering these issues, and clarifying your own position.

Statements about religion, with the exceptions of the quotation drawn from the Pope's encyclical and the statement by Rabbi David Lapin, are drawn from the site /www.religioustolerance.org/euthanas.htm#chur/.

Appendices

The High Cost of Waiting

No one really wants to think about aging or illness, but a few moments considering your future could save a lot of money over the long run. *Basically, the longer one waits to buy long term care insurance, the more expensive it gets.*

Now, when I explained this to my daughter, she wondered, "But doesn't it work out to be the same? If I spend a smaller amount of money for a longer time, won't it be equivalent to a larger amount of money for a shorter time? Why should I start spending the money now?" If you have the same question, then this appendix is for you.

Let's consider an example of the high cost of waiting:

> John Doe purchases long term care insurance at age fifty-five. John (or Jane — the gender doesn't matter!) is married and healthy, and rated by underwriting as a preferred risk. Policy benefits purchased are:
>
> - a daily facility benefit of $150,
> - a daily home care benefit of $150,
> - a lifetime benefit period,
> - a five percent annually compounded inflation protection rider, and
> - a twenty-day elimination period.

The premiums quoted below are for the client only (not including the spouse). They do, however, reflect a spousal discount, which is available from this company even if only one spouse applies. You can view the chart below or the summary that follows.

The Cost of Waiting

The following table summarizes the costs of waiting to purchase this long term care policy with a daily benefit of $150.

Age	Risk Category*	Daily Benefit**	Annual Premium	Total Premium to Age 90	Cost of Waiting
55	Preferred	$150	$2,325	$81,375	$0
65	Standard	$244	$7,239	$180,973	$99,598
75	Standard	$398	$29,211	$438,163	$257,190

*The likelihood of obtaining a standard rate declines with age. At ages 65 and 75 many applicants are offered substandard rates, meaning that their premiums would be higher than those shown here.

**At ages 65 and 75, the daily benefit reflects the impact of inflation on initial premiums. Increases in benefits result from a compound 5 percent inflation factor; thus, the premiums shown are buying the level of benefits equivalent to that if a $150 daily benefit was purchased at age 55. Note that actual costs of long term care are currently inflating at a rate even greater than 5 percent.

If the Policy Is Purchased at Age Fifty-Five

The annual premium would be $2,325, which would buy $150/day of benefits. **Total premium payments to age ninety would equal $81,375.** Now compare that with the cost of waiting ten more years to buy the same level of benefits.

If the Policy Is Purchased at Age Sixty-Five

Let's say John or Jane waited until age sixty-five to purchase the policy. In that case, the annual premium would be $7,239 to buy a benefit of $244 a day. ($244 a day is equal to the benefit that the person who bought at fifty-five would enjoy, considering the effects of 5% compound inflation to that point.) **Total premium payments to age ninety would equal $180,973.** These figures assume that John is still insurable, and can get a standard rating. Time to make a move, because…

If the Policy Is Purchased at Age Seventy-Five

The annual premium would be $29,211 to buy a benefit of $398 a day. (This is the same benefit that the person who bought at age fifty-five would have, considering the effects of 5 percent compound inflation over those years.) **Total premium payments to age ninety would equal $438,163.** Again, these figures assume that John is still insurable, and can still get a standard rating.

Which figure would you rather pay? Would you prefer paying $81,375 starting at fifty-five, $180,973 starting at sixty-five, or $438,163 at seventy-five? In a perfect world, you would never get old, never get sick, never need care… but until that day comes, it's clear that the sooner you start your long term care investment, the more money you'll have available for everything else!

Why an Inflation Rider Is a Must

When purchasing LTCI, it is vital to add an inflation rider. Without it, inflation can erode the usefulness of the policy. Two hundred dollars a day of care may sound great in current dollars, but by the time you or your loved one actually begins to collect under the policy, decades may pass. Twenty years from now, $200 a day may buy precious little. Just think about what inflation has done to the "value of a dollar" in your own lifetime… I'm not the only one who remembers three-cent stamps!

There are two kinds of insurance riders — compound inflation and simple inflation. *Compound inflation is absolutely necessary for buyers seventy or younger.* If you are over seventy and you can find an affordable policy with compound inflation, by all means buy it! This is the best protection you can have to maintain the value of your insurance investment. If you can't buy a policy that offers compound inflation, then at a minimum purchase a simple inflation rider — or your benefits may be dangerously low (relatively speaking) by the time you need them.

The following chart compares the two kinds of inflation, and demonstrates just how beneficial inflation riders really are.

Comparing the Growth of $200 Per Day in Benefits
Increasing at 5% Compound vs. 5% Simple Inflation

Year	Compound	Simple	Year	Compound	Simple
1	$200	$200	31	$864	$500
2	210	210	32	908	510
3	221	220	33	953	520
4	232	230	34	1001	530
5	243	240	35	1051	540
6	255	250	36	1103	550
7	268	260	37	1158	560
8	281	270	38	1216	570
9	295	280	39	1277	580
10	310	290	40	1341	590
11	326	300	41	1408	600
12	342	310	42	1478	610
13	359	320	43	1552	620
14	377	330	44	1630	630
15	396	340	45	1711	640
16	416	350	46	1797	650
17	437	360	47	1887	660
18	458	370	48	1981	670
19	481	380	49	2080	680
20	505	390	50	2184	690
21	531	400	51	2293	700
22	557	410	52	2408	710
23	585	420	53	2529	720
24	614	430	54	2655	730
25	645	440	55	2788	740
26	677	450	56	2927	750
27	711	460	57	3073	760
28	747	470	58	3227	770
29	784	480	59	3389	780
30	823	490	60	$3558	$790

Appendix C

What Is a Nursing Home?
What Is an Assisted Living Facility?

When I talk about living options for older people, there is always some definition of terms required. There are so many facilities, and sometimes it seems that every facility has another title, another name.

"Nursing homes" include convalescent homes, convalariums, and sanatariums. Nursing homes are group-living facilities offering medically supervised care for people who need assistance with their daily living (in activities like walking, eating, dressing, bathing, toileting, or supervision for substantial memory loss or dementia). The staff of a nursing home consists of aides, certified nursing assistants, administrators, and nurses. There must be easy access to doctors when required, and every resident must be seen by a doctor at least once a month.

"Assisted living facilities" include board-and-care homes, and residential care facilities. Residential care facilities provide rooms, meals, and activities for people independently able to care for most of their own daily needs. Those who live in residential care facilities are free to come and go as they wish, setting their own schedule. Residential care facilities are not required to have doctors or nurses on staff, but they may contract with a home health care agency for medical care (for example, doctor or nurse house calls in case of illness), and they may offer assistance in basic activities of daily living, such as dressing and bathing. Residential care facilities are usually *not* licensed to house any person who requires significant medical care or assistance with daily living.

Why Affluent People Should Consider Buying Long Term Care Insurance

by David Donchey, CLU

Often I am asked, "What is the typical financial profile of a long term care insurance prospect? Is it someone with $50,000 in assets? $500,000? $1,000,000? Or more?" Most insurance companies target prospects with estate values ranging from $75,000 to $750,000 — any less and they assume the prospect probably can't afford to buy the insurance; any more and they suggest that the prospect can most likely self-insure.

Although there are a number of important objective standards in measuring the financial suitability of a potential buyer of long term care insurance (LTCI), it is still rather subjective and open to individual agent interpretation and buyer demand. For example, adult children may want to purchase LTCI for a parent who, without the financial aid of the children, might not be able to afford the insurance otherwise. That purchase and the issue of suitability may be less about asset protection and more about self-reliance, dignity, avoiding Medicaid, and the shifting of caregiver responsibilities. Conversely, someone with a $5,000,000 estate would probably not need to buy LTCI insurance, but may want to buy it because of a variety of personal, financial, and logical factors.

Most people are surprised when I respond to that opening question with, "Anyone who can afford the premiums should consider buying LTCI." Anyone?

Including successful, affluent people? Absolutely. On the surface, this appears to be incongruous with traditional LTCI buying "tips." Most people believe the mantra that people with large estates should "self-insure" the costs of long term care, and "don't need to throw their money away on LTCI." (I define a large estate as one with assets of over two million dollars.)

Perhaps wealthy people don't need LTCI, but when presented with realistic facts, they might want it because it seems logical and makes common sense. Before you decide that you don't need to purchase LTCI because your assets exceed artificial barometers, consider the following points:

Averages don't apply to "above-average" wealth. Although average annual long term care costs hover around $60,000 in 2002, successful people should be cautious about thinking in terms of "averages." Wealthy people are generally accustomed to having higher standards of living, better lifestyles, and access to finer things — including better health care. They are likely to spend whatever it takes to get the best and most appropriate care possible. Most LTCI policies provide the insured with freedom of choice when it comes to determining who the providers are and how much to pay them — hence, the ability to hire the best care providers. Discussing "average daily" or "average annual" LTC costs may be counterproductive for those who are successful. Pay particular attention to high-end costs, which commonly run $120,000 to $300,000 per year. Full-time, round-the-clock unskilled care can easily cost $15.00-$20.00 per hour — or around $360.00-$480.00 per day. Add to that the cost of physical and speech therapy, and you quickly reach those higher numbers.

You worked hard for the money. Wealthy people generally don't end up wealthy by accident. Wealth accumulation is usually a result of a lifetime of hard work, good decisions, and perhaps a little luck. As people age, they tend to become more financially conservative. Achieving and maintaining financial success includes taking advantage of leverage opportunities, something that LTCI policies offer. Poor financial decision making is generally not in the fabric of successful people, and a well thought-out plan for LTC needs should be no different. These are people who already insure practically every other significant risk they're faced with (they would never think of dropping their health insurance!). The majority of this risk can be transferred out of an estate using interest from investments instead of using principal.

There's no place like your home. The relatively recent development of LTCI policies in California (and other states as well) includes many consumer protection features, and policies will pay outstanding benefits for home care that better allow people to remain in their own home in the event they need care. No one wants to be institutionalized, but it takes money, sometimes a lot of it, to pay for full-time care in one's own home. Liquid resources (like LTCI) provide markedly increased leverage opportunities, regardless of net worth.

Asset protection does matter. Current LTCI policies can provide significant asset protection, even to affluent people. Most plans offer a lifetime (unlimited) benefit period and many offer daily benefits of up to $300 to $500 per day. That's $109,500 to $182,500 of benefits per year in today's dollars! *Add in a 5 percent compound inflation rider and those insurance benefits will double by the end of the fourteenth policy year.* Conversely, choosing to self-insure can end up being a financially painful and wasteful mistake for the high net-worth couple. In the event that one or both spouses need care, it can become a drain on the estate that will get everyone's attention. It's just not a smart use of money when a charity or heirs would have been better off, not to mention the peace of mind the insurance offers. Since people tend to think in terms of "today's dollars"; be sure to factor in the ongoing rising costs of LTC (averaging about 7 percent per year over the past fifteen years). Wealthy people may recognize LTCI as a simple estate preservation technique that is part of the legacy they are already attempting to create. It can also help avoid having to one day say, "If only we had…"

Do the math. Based on current figures, a $13,000 combined annual premium for two 65-year-olds represents approximately only 1/4 of 1 percent of their $5,000,000 estate — a small price to pay in order for each of them to protect $109,500 ($300 daily benefit) per year, compounding for the rest of their lives. They only use about 1/4 of 1 percent of their estate… but in return they get 100 percent peace of mind.

Who's on first? In addition to asset protection afforded by LTCI policies, some policies have features that offer services important to anyone — rich or otherwise — faced with a long term care situation. Becoming chronically ill or disabled at any age is a real crisis for a family, and most people wouldn't know the first thing to do or whom to call to help orchestrate the services required when a family member is stricken with a catastrophic illness. LTCI policies may include care coordination services that provide appropriate levels of support and assistance that anyone, including affluent people, need in a crisis situation. Care coordinators gather, coordinate, and recommend many of the necessary services that chronically ill people require. These LTCI policy benefits help family members concentrate their efforts and energy on making sure their loved one is as comfortable as possible, as opposed to having to be the ones to navigate the labyrinth of issues involved in drafting and implementing a long term care plan. For those who purchase LTCI policies without care coordination, plan on hiring a geriatric care manager independently to help in a crisis situation or on an ongoing basis.

Tell me, what's your plan? A long term care insurance policy is, in fact, part of a bona fide plan. What's *your* written plan in case of a stroke, accident, Alzheimer's diagnosis, severe arthritis, or some other chronic ailment? It shouldn't surprise you that most people don't have one. Most people who decide not to purchase LTCI subsequently fail to design or create an alternative written plan that defines a course of action in case of catastrophic illness or injury. A high-quality LTCI policy can be a significant part of the solution to the problem of not having a written plan in case of a stroke or other disease or injury that makes it difficult to function independently. A long term care insurance policy can be combined with a professionally drafted, written document that clearly expresses the location where care should be received. Without it, individuals (and their families) will most likely be dealing with personal crises in a way that may contradict what they want and thought would probably happen. The bottom line? People can pay a relatively small amount for a policy and written plan now, or they can wait and end up with a potentially substantial financial and emotional cost later on.

It's tax deductible. Many successful people have corporations or other business entities that can pay the premium on their (and their spouse's) individually owned tax qualified LTCI policy(ies). Based on current tax law, a business may take advantage of a full or partial tax deduction of the premium, and policy benefits are still received tax free. Future LTC needs can be funded with tax-deductible dollars, premiums do not have to be declared as income, and benefits can be received income tax free. (Be sure to consult with a professional tax adviser for advice on tax issues.)

What do other advisers say? Business managers, CPAs, and attorneys are often concerned about protecting their high-profile clients' financial interests, especially when tax-deductible dollars can be used. (In fact, many highly successful clients often show an interest in purchasing LTCI on their parents' lives once they are aware of the potential benefits available.) These "centers of influence" are interested in learning more about LTC issues and will typically advise their clients to purchase LTCI.

Why pay premiums forever? Since affluent people generally have the money, it may be easier to pay the premiums for an LTCI policy in a shorter period of time. Examples are a ten-pay option or payments made to age sixty-five. Once the policy owner pays his/her respective final payment, the policy can become paid up and guaranteed against any future premium increases that may be applied to that particular block of business. When a business entity (primarily a C-corporation) is available to pay the premiums as cited above, the tax deductions further reduce the insured's cost and make the concept even more appealing.

In closing, there is no "typical" high-end financial profile of a long term care insurance buyer. It can and does include high net-worth people, especially once they or their advisers recognize the value these products have to offer.

When considering the purchase of long term care insurance, be sure to select an agent with experience. Choose an agent who represents several highly rated insurance companies that have experience offering this type of coverage. Ask the agent about any special training courses they've taken, designations they've earned, and any personal experiences they may have had with long term care. You may also want to ask the agent if he or she personally owns a long term care insurance policy. One would hope that they practice what they preach!

David Donchey, CLU, is the director of Long Term Care Insurance Sales and senior vice president of Leisure Werden & Terry, a brokerage general agency.

Care Management Trusts

By Ferd H. Mitchell and Cheryl C. Mitchell

Almost all people are concerned about what might happen to them if a major illness strikes. What will happen, they ask, if I am unable to care for myself? Who will look after me? Who will make certain that I receive the care I need and pay my bills?

Few people have family members who can move in with them and provide the needed care. Even if a child lives in the same city, he or she may not be able to move in with the parent. Children may have families and careers of their own. Frequently, family members are not even in the same city or state. In such cases, it may be impossible for a family member to provide the necessary care.

Often, a parent does not want to move into the home of the child, but prefers to stay at home and keep his or her independence. For individuals experiencing memory problems (such as Alzheimer's disease or dementia), remaining in one's own home provides both familiar surroundings and comfort, as an added value.

While we originally developed the first *care management trust* for a person who had no relatives, various types of trust versions have now been created for many different circumstances. These trusts have been developed for the following situations: married couples planning together, a married person with an ill spouse, a single person planning for the future, and a single person who has a disabled child. Trusts may be prepared for all individuals who have children either unwilling or unable to assist their parents.

While living trusts have been around for many years, typical trusts provide only for payment of expenses and investment of funds. Usually, a bank or other business trustee is appointed to handle the finances of the person who sets up the trust. A Care Management Trust is a much more effective approach to making sure that future care needs will be met in the best way.

Understanding Care Management Trusts

When a trust is established, the person who sets up the trust is known as the trustor. The person or persons that the trust is set up to benefit are known as the beneficiaries. The person who is responsible for carrying out the terms of the trust is known as the trustee.

There may be more than one trustee. For example, in a Care Management Trust, the person who looks after the personal care needs of the beneficiary is known as the personal care trustee. The person or company who is responsible for paying bills and managing money is the financial management trustee.

There may also be a trust monitor, to make sure that the trust is carried out the way the trustor intended. The trust monitor can also resolve questions or disagreements between the financial management trustee and the personal care trustee. For a Care Management Trust, arrangements must be made to take care of the needs of the beneficiary. This means that someone must be involved closely with the beneficiary, to know what his or her needs are. If there is no family member who can do this, or if a family member is too far away, then someone must be able to visit with the beneficiary on a regular basis.

The Care Management Trust clearly defines the responsibilities of the personal care trustee. The trust makes it clear that the duties of the financial management trustee are not the same as those of the personal care trustee; while it is possible to name one person to carry out both tasks, usually this is not preferred.

The Personal Care Trustee

A child may be able to pay the bills, but he or she may not have the training or time to actually manage the caregivers on a daily basis. Generally, the job of arranging for and supervising the care is assigned to a personal care trustee. The personal care trustee may be a care manager. Care managers are usually trained as social workers, and are tuned in to meeting the personal care needs of a beneficiary.

The duty of a care manager is to make sure that the daily needs of the beneficiary are being met. The care manager should be responsible for hiring the individuals who provide care to the beneficiary. He or she will be able to run background checks and assess the care being provided. The care manager will also arrange for medical care, dental care, and social outings.

If modifications to the beneficiary's home are necessary, the care manager will arrange for the necessary changes. For example, if the beneficiary is in a wheelchair, he or she may need to have the bathroom made accessible. In addition, if the doorways are too small for a wheelchair to pass through, the care manager can decide whether to buy a smaller wheelchair for inside the house, or consider whether it will be necessary to widen the doorways.

Care managers generally do not handle the financial affairs of the beneficiary. Their only interest is in making sure that the needs of the beneficiary are met in the best way. Care managers are now a nationally recognized profession and many belong to the National Academy of Professional Geriatric Care Managers.

The Financial Management Trustee

The care management trust must also provide for someone to handle the finances of the trustor or beneficiary. If the beneficiary is not able to pay bills and make investment decisions, then these tasks pass to the financial management trustee. These trustees do not make care decisions; they only handle financial matters.

One of the problems with traditional trusts is that a financial management trustee may feel obligated to keep expenses down so that there will be money left over when the beneficiary passes away. This can create a lot of problems, because under this type of trust, the financial management trustee may not be willing to spend money for the beneficiary even if the money is needed for this person's welfare.

Therefore, when preparing a care management trust, the person establishing the trust may wish to include the requirement: *"Don't save money for the people who will inherit it, if it will deprive me of quality care."* The trust can require that the needs of the beneficiary be considered first, before the interests of those who will inherit the money. Under a typical trust, if a beneficiary needs to have the doorways widened, the financial management trustee might say, "I won't pay for that. Just don't go into the rooms where the wheelchair will not fit through the doorway." With a care management trust, the beneficiary's needs come first.

A person can establish a trust for his or her own benefit. If this happens, the trustor and the beneficiary are one and the same person. A husband and wife can set up a trust together. Also, a husband can establish a care management trust for himself and his wife; the trustor is the husband and both he and his wife are the beneficiaries. Why would a husband want to set up a trust for his wife?

> Megan has been diagnosed with Alzheimer's disease and her husband, James, has been diagnosed with prostate cancer. He believes he will be able to care for his wife for as long as he lives (which he expects to be for many years). But if he dies before she does, who will look after her?
>
> He has promised her that he will never put her in a nursing home. James wants to make sure that she is well cared for at home for as long as she lives. His son, their only child, is a successful engineer in another state, and is not able to move home to take care of his mother.

There are many reasons for setting up a care management trust. A child might wish to set up such a trust for a parent. A parent might want to set up a trust for a disabled child. It is easy to imagine the different situations that could come up where a regular trust would not work as desired.

In regular trusts, the financial management trustee is not required to visit the beneficiary. In many cases, individuals who are beneficiaries of such trusts are placed in nursing homes or other care facilities. The trustee then assumes that the facility will provide for the needs of the beneficiary. The trustee will pay the bills as they come in.

But who actually looks after the needs of a nursing home resident? Many people assume that the nursing home will do this. Nursing home workers have very little time for individual attention to particular residents. Staff members who have many patients to care for do the basics of bathing, feeding, and dressing. Meals are prepared for dozens (if not hundreds) of residents at one time. There is no individual cooking for a particular resident.

Doctors' visits in the nursing home are generally done by a physician who visits the resident once a month. If residents are ill, they may not receive prompt medical attention. Very few dentists visit nursing homes, and dental care will have to be arranged by the nursing home social worker, if at all.

Most people want to live in their own homes as long as possible. For people who have the funds to do this, it is generally the best choice. If there is enough money to pay for this kind of care, the individual can remain at home with personal, professional caregivers. If a person does not have enough money to pay for home care, then purchasing a long term care insurance policy will help pay for the care. Costs can be paid for privately, through insurance, or by a combination of personal funds and insurance. There are often other types of alternative facilities available, if home care is not possible. It is important to make the best arrangements for each person on an individual basis.

Questions and Answers

Question: Can I prepare a care management trust for myself?
Answer: Yes, you can.

Question: How can I do this?
Answer: When you set up the trust, you can name yourself as the trustor *and* trustee. You can name an alternate personal care trustee and financial management trustee who will take over if you are not able to carry out the duties of the trust.

Question: Can I change the people I have named as alternate trustees?
Answer: Yes, you can, unless you have made your trust *irrevocable*. The word "irrevocable" means that you agree not to make any changes in your trust in the future.

Question: Where can I have a care management trust prepared?
Answer: Your attorney should be able to prepare this type of trust for you. He or she can obtain sample care management trusts from

the book *Elder Law and Practice with Forms,* volume 26 of *Washington Practice,* published by West Group, which was written by the authors of this article. Books can be ordered from West Group at (800) 221-9428. West Group maintains a Web site at: /www.westgroup.com/. If your attorney subscribes to *WestLaw,* a legal information Internet site operated by West Group, he or she can find the sample trusts online.

(The above-mentioned book is written for lawyers and does not contain forms that can be used by the general public. Setting up a care management trust is complicated, and it is important to have an attorney guide you through the procedure.)

Issues to Consider Before Setting Up a Care Management Trust

Who is the person setting up the trust?
    Answer: It can be you, you and your spouse, or someone else.

For whose benefit is the trust being set up?
    Answer: This can be you, you and your spouse, or someone else.

How long do you want the trust to last?
    Answer: Generally, the trust should last for the lifetime of the beneficiary, but you may put a time limit on it.

How do you want the trust funds used? Are there limits on what you should want the funds to be used for? Are there certain things for which you should say that trust funds *must* be used?
    Answer: If, for example, it is your desire to avoid being moved to a nursing home, then you can say that funds must be used to keep you in your own home. If you are concerned that the financial management trustee will think that the least expensive type of care will do, then you can specify that you do not want the cheapest care, but the kind of care that allows you to remain in your own home.

Do you want to have any money given away from the trust?

Answer: If, for example, you always give your children $500 each year for Christmas, you may not want to continue these gifts, especially if you might not be able to pay your own bills.

Should I establish a Care Management Trust (CMT) in case I later need to qualify for Medicaid?

Answer: Medicaid is a joint federal-state program that pays for nursing home care for persons who do not have funds to pay for their own care. A Care Management Trust should not be prepared by a person who has limited funds and may need to qualify for Medicaid.

What will happen to any funds that remain in the trust when you (or another beneficiary) pass away?

Answer: If you have established a trust for yourself, then you can name the person or persons who will receive any remaining funds when you die. If you have established a trust for yourself and your spouse, then you can state that the trust will continue until both you and your spouse pass away. Then you can name the person or organizations that will receive any funds that remain.

What about estate tax planning?

Answer: Estate tax planning can be included with a care management trust, so you can both protect yourself (and your spouse), and make the best use of opportunities to minimize taxes that will be due when you pass away.

APPENDIX F

Essential Phone Numbers

Our Web site, /www.LongTermCareLA.com/, offers links to these and other referral sources to assist you in your planning.

Long Term Care Insurance:

Karen Shoff, MSW, MSG, LUTCF, may be reached at (310) 581-8080; or through her Web site at /www.LongTermCareLA.com/; or by e-mail at: Karen@LongTermCareLA.com.

Geriatric Care Managers:

The National Association of Geriatric Care Managers lists more than nine hundred members in their directory, available for $15. The association may be contacted through their Web site at /www.caremanager.org/, by writing to them at 1604 N. Country Club Road, Tucson, AZ 85716, or by calling them at (520) 881-8008.

Senior Outreach Services of the Jewish Family Service of Los Angeles is a nonprofit, nonsectarian organization that offers care-coordination services (geriatric care management). Senior Outreach Services may be contacted at (323) 937-6275 or sosjfsla@earthlink.net.

Halachic living wills:

Agudath Israel of America: (212) 797-9000
Rabbinical Council of America: (212) 807-7888

Care Management Trust Forms:

Your lawyer can access the *westlaw* Web site if they subscribe to it, and search in Volume 26 of *Washington Practice* to find the sample forms.

Contacting Contributors to This Book

Steven Barlam is the president of the National Association of Professional Care Managers and chief professional officer and cofounder of *LivHOME*, an eldercare solutions company committed to enabling older clients to live at home longer with maximum comfort, safety, dignity, and respect. *LivHOME* is based in Los Angeles, with three offices serving Santa Barbara, Ventura, Los Angeles, and Orange Counties. *LivHOME* may be reached at (877) 454-8466 or through their Web site at /www.livhome.com/.

David Donchey, CLU, is director of Long Term Care Insurance Sales and senior vice president of *Leisure Werden & Terry*, a brokerage general agency with offices in Pasadena and San Francisco. David Donchey can be reached at (800) 272-2212, ext. 240, or by e-mail at davedonchey@lwtagency.com.

Anne Hanssen, MSG, is director of *Gerontology Home Companion*, a home care aide organization located in Woodland Hills, California. She can be reached at (818) 713-0640.

Ferd H. Mitchell and Cheryl C. Mitchell, husband and wife attorneys, have developed Care Management Trusts in response to requests by clients. They practice together at Mitchell Law Office in Spokane, Washington, and may be reached at (509) 327-5181. They have been working together on programs and activities on behalf of the elderly for over twenty-five years.

Stephen A. Moses is president of the *Center for Long Term Care Financing*, a 501(c)(3) nonprofit charitable organization in Bellevue, Washington. He was formerly a Medicaid state representative for the Health Care Financing Administration, and a senior analyst for the Office of Inspector General of the United States Department of Health and Human Resources. He is widely recognized as an expert and innovator in the field of long term care.

The *Center for Long Term Care Financing* is committed to the challenge of educating financial professionals about long term care and the necessary means to prepare for that risk. Its mission is to ensure quality long term care for all Americans. It pursues this objective by encouraging public policy that targets scarce public resources to the genuinely needy and provides incentives to everyone else to save, invest, or insure for the risk of long term care. Readers may consult numerous studies, speeches, and other publications at /www.centerltc.org/, and subscribe to LTC Bullets, their free online newsletter, by filling out the form on the Web site or dropping a note with contact information, including e-mail address, to info@centerltc.org.

Caren R. Nielsen is a partner at Glantz, Nielsen, Gillin & Scott, where she practices elder law, estate planning, probate, and conservatorships. You may contact her concerning elder law or any area of estate planning that applies to your personal needs at (818) 501-3100, by visiting /www.gngslaw.com/, by e-mail at crn@gngslaw.com, or at 15760 Ventura Blvd., #1520, Encino, CA 91436.

Judith Tobenkin, MS, MSG, Certified Care Manager, is located in Beverly Hills, California. She may be reached at (310) 273-3548 or by e-mail at jtobenkin@aol.com.

REFERENCES

1. Lucette Lagnado, "Living and Dying: An Innovative New Jersey Program Offers What May Be a More Humane Alternative to Nursing Homes," *Wall Street Journal* (February 21, 2001): R11.

2. Health Insurance Association of America, *Long-Term Care: Knowing the Risk, Paying the Price,* 1997.

3. Kimberly Lankford, "Arm Yourself While You Can," *Kiplinger's* (March 2001): 98. The surveys were conducted by LifePlans, a research firm, for the Robert Wood Johnson Foundation and the Federal Department of Health and Human Services.

4. Ann Davis, *Wall Street Journal* (June 22, 2000).

5. Richard Schulz, Ph.D. and Scott R. Beach, Ph.D, Caregiving As a Risk Factor for Mortality, *Journal of the American Medical Association* 282, no. 23 (December 15, 1999).

   see also: "Elder Care Hard on Givers, Study Finds," *Los Angeles Daily News* (March 27, 1998), reporting on a Stanford University study.

6. *The MetLife Juggling Act Study on Balancing Caregiving with Work and the Costs Involved.* This study was completed in November 1999 and includes findings from a national study by the National Alliance for Caregiving and the National Center on Women and Aging at Brandeis University. For more information on this study, contact the Mature Market Institute MetLife at (203) 221-6580 or e-mail: MMI_MetLife@metlife.com.

7. *New York Times* (May 7, 2000).

8. Richard Atcheson, "Our Old House," *Modern Maturity* (November-December 2000): 70, 73.

9. Neergaard, Lauren, "Deathly Ill Patients Want Options, Including Euthanasia," *Associated Press* (November 14, 2000).

   see also: Journal of the American Medical Association, December 20, 2000.

This Exciting Book Might Save Your Life —
and the Lives of Those You Love the Most!

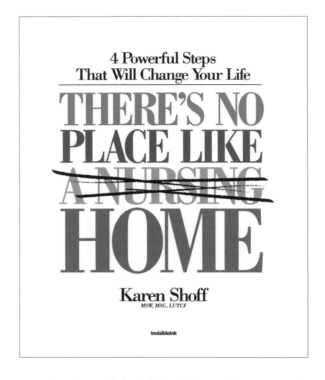

To Order This Life-Changing Book:

Order Online: www.LongTermCareLA.com
Phone toll-free: 1-800-BOOKLOG (1-800-266-5564)
. . .or contact your local bookseller.
For bulk sales and information on orders by mail or fax,
    call toll-free: (866) 582-5222.

Copies of THERE'S NO PLACE LIKE (A NURSING) HOME are available for $12.95 each,
plus shipping and handling. (Ohio and California residents please add sales tax.)

To contact the author about seminars or speaking engagements,
    call (310) 581-8080 or e-mail Karen@LongTermCareLA.com.